Dear Monika

Good Luck with your journey

as a Leader of Quality

Ron

★★★★★

LEADING
QUALITY

How Great Leaders

DELIVER HIGH-QUALITY

SOFTWARE AND

ACCELERATE GROWTH

Jun 24.

RONALD CUMMINGS-JOHN • OWAIS PEER

PRAISE FOR LEADING QUALITY

"A quality mindset remains key to differentiating your product and your company. *Leading Quality* offers key lessons to develop this mindset."
Michael Lopp, author of *Managing Humans* and VP of Product Engineering at Slack

"Three elements define any successful product: quality, quality, and quality. *Leading Quality* is a comprehensive and practical guide to embedding quality into the DNA of any product organization."
Nick Caldwell, CPO at Looker and former VP of Engineering at Reddit

"Every crisis of quality begins as a crisis of leadership. *Leading Quality* will help you avoid both kinds of trouble."
James Bach, author of *Lessons Learned in Software Testing*

"*Leading Quality* provides a fascinating insight to help guide leaders in their journey to implement effective QA strategies, particularly when delivering high-quality products in IT."
Ilya Sakharov, Director of QA at HelloFresh

"*Leading Quality* is a must-read for all managers who are serious about quality within their organizations. From automation to best practices and insights, this book covers it all."
Maryann Lockley, Head of QA at Camelot Group - The National Lottery

"Finally! A book to help managers and executives understand why they should care about quality and why a big investment in quality pays off in the form of a successful product. Insights and stories from leading quality practitioners illustrate why and how companies need to focus on quality."

Lisa Crispin, author of *Agile Testing* and *More Agile Testing*

"If you are a manager contemplating automated or continuous testing, there are valuable insights within these pages."

Robert Martin, author of *The Clean Coder*

"Most books in this space just focus on the details of testing, this is the first book that tells you how to LEAD quality."

Daniel Knott, author of *Hands-On Mobile App Testing*

"*Leading Quality* stands out as one of the few titles that actually talks about how to lead quality from a manager's perspective. A great read for those who want to take their team to the next level."

Stephen Janaway, VP Engineering at Bloom & Wild

"While testers already have an intuitive and instinctive grasp of why quality is important for their organizations, many of them have a hard time explaining this concept in a way that inspires attention, motivation, or action in their C-Level colleagues. This is where *Leading Quality* comes in. It's full of interesting examples and useful ways to articulate why quality is important and how it can help your company."

Vernon Richards, Managing Director at House of Test (UK), conference host & speaker

"Quality software will never happen from testing alone. The highest-quality software comes from teams and organizations that have a culture of quality and achieving a culture of quality requires strong quality leadership. This excellent book from Ron and Owais interweaves stories about quality and leadership with pragmatic advice and research that anyone can use to lead quality in their own organizations."

Alan Page, Quality Director at Unity Technologies and co-host of the AB Testing podcast

"For too long, there has been a disconnect between testers and C-level leaders in terms of how testing and quality are viewed. This book is a MUST-READ for anyone in a management or leadership position. *Leading Quality* is also a useful resource for testers as it gives different perspectives on quality and will equip you with the language to be able to speak to the managers and leaders in your organization to positively influence change. This book is only the beginning of a big movement toward quality leadership within the industry."

Dan Ashby, Head of Quality Engineering at Photobox and former Head of Testing at eBay

"*Leading Quality* will help QA professionals advocate for investing in quality at any stage of a company's growth by illustrating why quality matters through frameworks and insights from some of the leading practitioners in tech."

Suyash Sonwalkar, Quality and Automation Lead at Coinbase

DOWNLOAD
THE AUDIOBOOK FREE!*

You can now become an industry leader in quality no matter how busy you are, with the official *Leading Quality* audiobook! Enjoy bonus insights, chapter commentary, and much more as coauthor Ronald Cummings-John takes you through the book, giving you the full *Leading Quality* experience.

Download now:
lqbook.co/audio

Leading Quality: How Great Leaders Deliver High-Quality Software and Accelerate Growth

Version 1.0.3

Published in Great Britain by ROI Press

ISBN 978-1-9161858-0-7 (Print)
ISBN 978-1-9161858-1-4 (ePub)
ISBN 978-1-9161858-4-5 (Kindle)

Cover Design: Jason Anscomb

★★★★★

LEADING QUALITY

How Great Leaders

DELIVER HIGH-QUALITY

SOFTWARE AND

ACCELERATE GROWTH

RONALD CUMMINGS-JOHN • OWAIS PEER

CONTENTS

FOREWORD XII

INTRODUCTION 1

How a Failed Startup Pointed Us to the Opportunity of QA 3

Quality Leadership Starts with Quality Communication 5

What You're Going to Get out of This Book 7

SECTION I: BECOMING A LEADER OF QUALITY

1| HOW QUALITY LOST ITS VALUE 10

History Repeats Itself 11

The Effects of Poor Quality on the 3Cs: Customers,

    Company, and Career 13

Laying the Foundations for Leading Quality 15

Chapter 1 Summary (TL;DR) 18

2| THE POWER OF A QUALITY NARRATIVE 19

The Ownership Narrative 21

The "How to Test" Narrative 23

The Value Narrative 24

Uncovering Your Quality Narrative 27

Chapter 2 Summary (TL;DR) 29

3| LEADING A CULTURE OF QUALITY.. **30**

Know the Audience You Need to Influence 32

Create Empathy to Increase Alignment and Understanding............34

Support the Narrative with Evidence...............................36

Cultivate Internal Champions 38

Chapter 3 Summary (TL;DR) 39

SECTION II: MASTERING YOUR STRATEGIC QUALITY DECISIONS

4| FOUNDATIONS: MANUAL TESTING VS. AUTOMATION **41**

Behind the Curtain of Automation 43

Can You Automate Everything? 45

Should You Automate Everything?.................................48

Chapter 4 Summary (TL;DR) 50

5| HOW QUALITY CHANGES WITH PRODUCT MATURITY **51**

The Validation Stage: Product-Market Fit.........................53

The Predictability Stage: Creating a Stable
Infrastructure for Scale 55

The Scaling Stage: Minimizing Negative Impact
to Unlock Growth 57

Chapter 5 Summary (TL;DR) 60

**6| IMPROVING FEEDBACK LOOPS TO SUPERCHARGE
CONTINUOUS TESTING** **61**

The Real Definition of "Continuous Testing".......................63

Feedback Loops..64

The Four Ways to Improve Your Feedback Loops 67

Chapter 6 Summary (TL;DR) 70

7| INVESTING IN TESTING INFRASTRUCTURE **71**

Monitoring for Impact on Your Users.......................................73

Testing in Production..75

Testing in Production Too Soon 77

Chapter 7 Summary (TL;DR) 80

SECTION III: LEADING YOUR TEAM TO ACCELERATE GROWTH

8| ALIGN YOUR TEAM TO YOUR COMPANY GROWTH METRIC **82**

The One Metric That Drives All Others 84

How to Identify the Right Growth Metric for Your Team 86

How Your Growth Metric Impacts Testing.......................... 90

Chapter 8 Summary (TL;DR) 92

9| DRIVING GROWTH WITH LOCAL PERSONAS **93**

Local Personas – Knowing Who Your Customers Are 94

Finding Your Local Personas to Support Growth 95

Testing the Local Experience 97

Chapter 9 Summary (TL;DR) 101

10| LEADING QUALITY STRATEGY **102**

Step 1 – Setting the Vision..104

Step 2 – Assessing Your Starting Point 106

Step 3 – Working Out the Strategy 109

Chapter 10 Summary (TL;DR) 112

THIS IS ONLY THE BEGINNING..**113**

BONUS CHAPTER: THE FUTURE – AUTONOMOUS TESTING.......................**114**

HELP US PROMOTE THE MESSAGE OF LEADING QUALITY.........................**115**

KEY RESOURCES **116**

    Worksheets 116

    Resources by Chapter 117

    Recommended Blogs/Influencers 119

ABOUT THE AUTHORS **120**

ACKNOWLEDGEMENTS **121**

NOTES **124**

INDEX **131**

FOREWORD

BY NEIL BROWN, TESTING SERVICES PARTNER
AT DELOITTE CONSULTING

Years ago, testing was an overhead expense.

Today, it's the centerpiece of business strategy.

In financial services, for instance, it used to be that if your bank or insurance company's software wasn't delivering at the level you expected, you had the option to switch providers. However, switching entailed weeks or even months of effort and paperwork. When comparing the annoyance of an inconvenient application against the challenge of transitioning to a competitor, few felt it was worth the work. One tech titan in particular was infamous for limiting their amount of testing and releasing software with known issues because, despite them, the company knew users would come back for later updates. Their customers became, in effect, testers working for free.

Today's customers business or consumer won't stand for that. They have too many options that they can choose too easily. They can go buy a similar product, or perhaps even the same one, from dozens or hundreds of other providers. They can afford to be fickle.

The result is that companies can no longer afford failure in production and the ensuing impact on their consumers. As recently as six or seven years ago, financial services would prioritize speed to market, or the risk of a regulatory breach, over the user's experience. It has taken significant issues like customers not having access to their funds or institutions mistakenly paying parties twice to highlight the costs of those choices. In many cases, a customer experience issue costs more than a regulatory breach or a legal challenge. The quality and usability of the end product has become far more mission-critical and, therefore, a far greater business focus.

Originally, testing was just part of a systems engineering role. As the complexity of programs increased, however, the software development industry realized we needed a more rigorous approach to quality. Even as that need arose and was recognized, testing was still seen as being on the far right-hand side of the delivery lifecycle, something to be squeezed into the project. Many saw it as an overhead to be ignored when at all possible.

I remember years ago going into an accounting software company and supporting them in developing their own testing practices and center of excellence. We faced enormous resistance because the rest of the organization didn't see the value. It's taken some fundamental shifts not only in development methodology but also in the mindset of companies for that to change. Now, testing and quality assurance have become central to what's happening.

QA isn't there to say that the product is ready to go. It's there to help understand the risk and the organization's risk profile. The earlier you can understand and articulate what that risk profile is, the better. That allows the business to then make informed decisions. Suddenly, quality becomes the key at the heart of any delivery cycle. We've witnessed the change and maturation of testing from being a phase in development to becoming a profession and then the key driver in the overarching delivery of change.

That's fundamentally changed the nature of the testing profession.

QA professionals must be able not only to mitigate risk but to translate its impact into words that drive behavior across the organization, from the developers to the executives.

It's not financially viable to deliver the same depth and breadth of testing today as we did on applications years ago. The complexity and sheer volume of code under test would require five or six times as much effort. It's simply not feasible from a resource perspective.

As testing has moved from the periphery of importance toward the center, the roles and required skills of our profession have changed, too. Being good at testing is no longer sufficient. Success now relies more and more on your ability to distill business insights from testing functions as well as to clearly articulate them and drive change across multiple teams.

"Leadership" for a QA professional encompasses more than just leading testing teams. If quality has become key to business success, then it stands to reason that those tasked with quality must be able to impact teams and contributors throughout the organization. You must be able to align with all the business teams while working within the overall goals and directions of the business, even as those environments constantly change.

A financial services company with a regulatory deadline might have one type of risk profile. An entertainment app might face intense market competition. A tech company might be preparing for a merger or acquisition. Each of these organizations presents a different profile of risk tolerance. It's now the responsibility of QA professionals to interpret those risk profiles and tailor their approach to testing accordingly.

In some circles, though, testing is still seen as a commodity a race to the bottom, using the cheapest resource available. In some cases, that is a valid approach, but I, for one, refuse to talk in terms of headcount and day rate. I talk about solutions, client value, and the risk mitigation achieved.

To do that, we at Deloitte combine both a deep technical knowledge base of development, solutions, and systems with an equally deep level of business expertise. We have experts in financial risk management, healthcare systems, SAP, Oracle, and others that we bring together to focus on the risks that matter to the business.

We're not interested in a client having to use us for four years because they've got nothing else they can do. We measure success on their not needing us. For instance, we had a four-year project with a client. At the end, they were self-sustaining; they didn't need Deloitte to continue supporting them. However, they chose to engage for another four years to support them on driving complex change and innovation in other parts of their business.

That type of outlook prioritizing client value over generating provider revenue is why we were attracted to Global App Testing (GAT). We were impressed that they were always pushing toward innovation. They didn't believe that just because the textbooks said to do something in particular, that made it right. GAT wasn't there just to provide services because that's what they were being paid for; they were there to deliver value and help maximize it.

What's been most heartening is the fact that, although we are a test consultancy that provides innovation and drives quality through our own consulting headcounts (contrasted against GAT's crowdsourced testing services), we found ways to complement each other in an end-to-end proposition whereby we can actually measure the cost of quality, and then use those measures to drive optimization through the functional testing process.

Being at the forefront of the testing industry, we've simply had to navigate these uncharted waters on our own. Despite the need, today's QA professionals have few resources to guide them in this new reality. That was my worry when Ronald and Owais told me about their book project. Perhaps this is an oversimplification, but every testing book I had found was written more from a theoretical perspective than one of practical experience.

Most of the books I've read focus on how to test better. We know how to test. What we need are pragmatic books based on hard-earned experience out in the real world that shows us how to deliver more value as QA professionals. Today's testers have to build relationships with everyone, from the development teams to the business teams. There aren't many resources to turn to that provide the tools to present ourselves in multiple styles to the various stakeholders throughout the delivery lifecycle. There aren't many resources that provide advice based on practical experience and real-world examples of how to manage, drive, and deliver quality in a complex business environment where communicating the risk associated with software quality is vitally important. We need those types of books.

Leading Quality is the first.

-Neil Brown, Testing Services Partner at Deloitte Consulting

INTRODUCTION

A single bug report forever changed the way we thought about QA.

Anna was an analyst working at a Swedish tech company experiencing incredible global growth. As she compared internal metrics among various countries, she saw that Indonesia lagged far behind the adoption rates of other Southeast Asian nations.

This wasn't particularly concerning at first. They had run into these kinds of country-specific issues before. Usually, they were able to iterate their way through the problem using analytics and monitoring tools. There was no reason to guess this would be any different.

She passed along the information to the product and engineering teams to look into the problem. However, as they began to A/B test different ideas to improve conversion rates, nothing moved the needle.

Anna reached out to us, asking if we could conduct a localized functional test in Indonesia, just to see if our team could find something they couldn't. When our local testers in Indonesia began running through the app, one of them flagged something we found odd: their bug report pointed out a problem with the "Last Name" field being compulsory during signup.

When Anna received the list of moderated bugs, she also thought this particular report was odd. Why wouldn't you enter a last name? That's how millions of users around the world register for new accounts every day. Why were things different in Indonesia?

When she did some research, she stumbled upon how big of an

issue this really was. She later explained to us what she had found: in Indonesia, just under 40% of the population don't have a last name.[1] This is a result of the 17,000 islands having over 300 different ethnic groups, in addition to hundreds of years of colonization, religion, and politics. While the more tech-savvy Indonesians work around this by typing a star or dot when prompted for their last name, other would-be users stop at this point.

The more she looked into it, the more she became convinced that the "Last Name" field was the true problem. She shared the information with her team and they made the change; Indonesia no longer required users to provide a last name on signup.

Once they made that change, an incredible thing happened: user adoption went through the roof, putting Indonesia ahead of all the other Southeast Asian countries.

Fixing that one bug had unlocked a market of 262 million people.

The company had been stumped by this problem for months. Their team in Sweden had racked their brains going through their internal data. It never once crossed their minds that something as simple as a last name was an issue, much less the primary barrier to adoption. It took a local tester to point out something that, to an Indonesian, was an obvious flaw.

When telling this story, I sometimes get asked "How can a company miss something so simple?" The truth is, in fast-paced organizations, both large and small, the simple things often get overlooked.

While it was great that this insight unlocked the growth they were looking for, perhaps the bigger impact was that, for the first time, senior people in Anna's company sat up and took notice of the value testing could provide.

Witnessing Anna's company go through this process had a profound effect on myself and my cofounder, Owais. We saw how testing could have a measurable impact on business growth. Wanting to know whether this was an outlier or not, we went looking for other examples with our clients and through our network of testing and tech professionals.

What we found fundamentally changed our perspective on how to lead quality. Leaders who had figured out how to leverage their quality teams to accelerate business growth had similar strategies and approaches to quality. Anna's story was just the tip of the iceberg.

As we dug deeper, many of the leaders we interviewed told us stories of how they had managed to turn around seemingly dire quality situations. These stories resonated with Owais and me...especially considering our own QA journey with our failed company, crippled by bad QA.

HOW A FAILED STARTUP POINTED US TO THE OPPORTUNITY OF QA

After spending the night reviewing the numbers, an awful, gut-wrenching conclusion washed over me: in order to survive, we had to pivot our business.

We had poured most of our seed investment into developing PS Beauty, a search engine for the beauty industry. Even though our London office was a drafty warehouse that got so cold you had to wear gloves to type, our excitement about building a company from nothing made up for our spartan surroundings. We'd often be so engrossed in our work we'd forget to eat. It didn't matter; we were high on the dream.

But launching a global search engine from scratch was far more complicated than the companies we'd built before. When I think back to our attempts to get it off the ground, I refer to it as "the fire era." Every day felt like we were running around trying to keep the "fires" from spreading while putting on a face to our customers as if everything was normal.

The "fire" that frustrated us the most was the number of bugs in our software. Owais and I would find bugs. Our engineers would find bugs. Our customers would find bugs. We soon realized that these quality issues were more than just problems—they were killing us. Our customers started getting frustrated because of the issues in our app, leading them to eventually abandon it altogether. Customers expected a seamless experience and our lack of quality ultimately strangled the company.

Our experience with PS Beauty is important because it reminds us that software issues aren't just inconveniences. They can kill applications, projects, or even whole companies like ours.

We founded Global App Testing to help other organizations deal with the same fires that killed our startup. We could empathize not only with our customers, but also with other companies; we knew that one of the latter's primary challenges lay in how they viewed testing. After all, we had first-hand experience of seeing a product fail precisely because of how we had approached QA.

As our company has grown, we have had the great fortune to work with and spend time inside companies. We saw what worked and what didn't for the leaders of those companies when it came to quality. We were commonly asked, "What should my QA strategy be?" Since we worked with that question almost every day, we didn't think it would take long to turn our thoughts into a book.

Little did we know it would take us on a two-and-a-half-year journey, meeting the top engineering, product, and QA leaders in the world from companies like Airbnb, Blackboard, Dell, Atlassian, Reddit, and other technology companies, totaling 120 interviews.

From our experience spending time with our testing community through more than sixty Testathon®, a hackathon-style event designed for testers, Owais and I also had the ability to expand and hone our ideas.

As we came to the end of the book, we realized that there was a much deeper question than, "What should my QA strategy be?" The question was, "How can I better lead quality inside my company?"

QUALITY LEADERSHIP STARTS WITH QUALITY COMMUNICATION

Engineering and quality leaders do a good job of telling a technical story, such as explaining the testing activities and how they plan to optimize the development process. Unfortunately, most miss the other side of the story, the part that clearly shows how the work they do adds value to their customers and contributes toward business growth. In order to be a great leader, it's important to understand and convey how these two factors relate to quality.

The word "quality," however, can be confusing. We all feel like we know what quality is. We know it's important. But it's actually not that easy to define in and of itself. To some people, it means reliability and efficiency. For others, it's fitness for purpose or usability. In fact, every single individual throughout your company may have a different way of defining this term.

When looking at various definitions of quality, there are two things that everyone seems to agree on:

1. Quality is subjective; it's determined by whoever is using the product at the time.
2. Quality is relative; it changes over time.

The reason it's so difficult to define is because each person defines it differently and continually changes that definition as each day passes. Michael Bolton said it best: "Quality is value to some person, at some time, who matters."[2]

For example, back when we first got the internet, we'd happily wait for five minutes for a page to load. We could go get a cup of coffee and sit back down, ready to read through the page. Today, we're used to pages loading in split seconds. If they don't, we get annoyed.

In the past, we were used to software crashing several times a day and having to deal with the awful Windows "blue screen of death." It frustrated us, but we put up with it because we had to. Nowadays, if something crashes, we just find the nearest competitor and start using their software instead. Our collective expectations of quality and tolerance of issues have shifted over time.

In his 2018 annual letter to shareholders,[3] Amazon founder Jeff Bezos talked about continual customer obsession as the key to Amazon's growth. According to Bezos, customers are always "divinely discontent." The customer's expectations never remain the same, their needs are forever growing, and their point of view is ever changing. They will always want something better than whatever they have today.

That's the essence of quality. It's hard to define because nothing about it is constant. But therein lies the opportunity in software development: by always trying to catch up with the moving goalposts of your customers' expectations, you will constantly be delivering better and higher-quality software.

Leaders who embrace this idea—that companies live and die by quality as perceived by their customers—and make it their mantra will adapt and grow with them. Those who focus on functionality and internal definitions of quality...won't.

WHAT YOU'RE GOING TO GET OUT OF THIS BOOK

The person in charge of leading quality inside a company can vary widely. In some companies, it's a strong mission led by the CEO. In others, it's the VP of Engineering, the Director of Quality, a product owner, or individual contributors not in a leadership role.

Whether you're a VP or a director looking to take your own leadership skills to the next level, a C-suite executive hoping to understand how you can have a better-quality product in your company, or an individual contributor trying to understand how you can make a difference in your company, there's something for you in all three sections of this book:

Section I: Becoming a Leader of Quality

This section teaches you how to influence internal views of quality, so that every layer of your company is aligned around delivering a great experience to your users. This alignment helps teams work closer together and feel more inspired. It also reduces the time needed to secure buy-in from the rest of management as well as members of your team. You might find yourself in situations where management doesn't understand why they need to invest in quality or that there is a general lack of appreciation for the importance of quality within the company. We will give you the framework that the best leaders use to influence and reset the way people think and talk about quality in their companies.

Section II: Mastering Your Strategic Quality Decisions

After reading this section, you will be more confident in the major strategic decisions you have to make when setting your quality strategy. We'll walk you through the experiences and thinking frameworks that the most successful leaders use to make decisions and point to indicators of what you'll have to think about as your product evolves. You will understand the factors behind the challenges, drivers, and outcomes that different strategic approaches have so you can alter your strategy as you lead.

Section III: Leading Your Team to Accelerate Growth

The final section of the book is dedicated to giving you the tools to ensure that your team is focused on the highest-impact activities that your organization cares about. We've seen great leaders accelerate growth in companies through their quality teams. Being able to successfully set and communicate an aligned quality strategy to your team may not just get you noticed; it could change your career.

The leadership ideas, tools and frameworks you're about to read have been proven to influence and create results for many of the top technology teams on the planet. We've managed to condense the last two and a half years of research and interviews into a short, three-hour read.

It may sound obvious, but the most successful leaders go to great lengths to improve themselves. We believe that, whether you're an aspiring leader or an industry veteran, you'll find several new insights in this book to shift the way you see and lead quality.

SECTION I

BECOMING A LEADER OF QUALITY

1│HOW QUALITY LOST ITS VALUE

"Every successful quality revolution has included the participation of upper management. We know of no exceptions."
Joseph M. Juran, author of *Juran's Quality Handbook*

During World War II, the UK had a problem: bombs exploding in the factories during manufacture. In response, the Ministry of Defence required all factories to have a written process for how they made their bombs and placed ministry-approved inspectors on-site to make sure those standards were adhered to. This became the catalyst for a movement toward "quality standards."

This solved the immediate problem. Bombs stopped exploding in the factories. (Or, at least, far fewer did.) But it didn't address other important issues: Did the bombs go off when they were supposed to (i.e., when being dropped on a target)? Was there a way of making better-quality bombs? Quality became solely focused on internal inspection, not value.

The next great leap in quality standards, however, came from an unexpected place: post-WWII Japan.

After the war, the nation's leaders looked to manufacturing and exporting finished goods as a way to quickly rebuild the devastated economy. But they took quality standards even further and developed new ideas, like "lean manufacturing"—a systematic method for eliminating waste within a manufacturing process—and kaizen, an approach for continuously improving their processes. These ideas focused on the flow of work through the production lines and the quality of the product.

From this came the concept of Total Quality Management (TQM), which flipped the whole perspective of quality on its head. Instead of focusing on just production, TQM defined quality as providing value to the customer.

Joseph M. Juran, one of the founding fathers of quality management and a mentor to Apple's Steve Jobs, authored *Juran's Quality Handbook*, in which he wrote the word "customer" 578 times. As corporations continued to look for a competitive advantage, having lean manufacturing processes and an optimized infrastructure for production became table stakes. They began to focus more on providing the kind of value through quality that Juran emphasized.

HISTORY REPEATS ITSELF

When the software industry was in its infancy, engineers modeled their work on best-practice manufacturing techniques, branching off from lean manufacturing and kaizen. These processes evolved into what we now call Agile development, lean principles, and DevOps. But, like manufacturing before it, the methods used focused heavily on improving the flow of code through the development process. This brought incredible speed improvements that helped software companies decrease the time it took to deliver products to market.

But that increase in speed came at a cost. Faster software deployments didn't always mean higher quality. As one DevOps consultant put it,[4] "Continuous deployment without quality is just delivering continuous bugs to your customers."

The testing platform Sauce Labs sponsored a survey of tech professionals that included a question about how quickly they would like to deploy: faster, the same, or slower?[5]

In 2016 no one said they wanted to slow down, but only 54% reported they wanted to deploy faster. When they released the same survey in 2017, something interesting happened: only 43% wanted to deploy faster, but 6% wanted to deploy slower. Then in 2018, 9% wanted to deploy slower.

HOW QUICKLY DO YOU WANT TO DEPLOY?			
	Faster	The Same	Slower
2016	54%	46%	0%
2017	43%	50%	6%
2018	44%	49%	9%

In an analysis of the results, the report read, "Perhaps development organizations have leaned too far into speed and now realize they need to bring quality back into the balance."[7]

Just like the journey the manufacturing industry took, focusing all of your efforts solely around optimizing for speed won't give you the long-term advantage you truly need. "Improving QA" has to be more than just eliminating the bottlenecks. It has to be about delivering quality as perceived by the customer.

THE EFFECTS OF POOR QUALITY ON THE 3CS:
CUSTOMERS, COMPANY, AND CAREER

Poor quality was estimated to have cost companies over $1.7 trillion in 2017. This is the equivalent of Canada's total GDP output for that year.[8] The fact that the global impact of bad QA equals the output of the tenth-largest economy in the world emphasizes the scale of the problem. Bringing the problem to a microlevel, the first people to be impacted when software goes wrong are usually your customers. Customer issues impact your company and company issues can impact your career.

We call these "the 3Cs."

We've all experienced an app freezing on our phone or not being able to complete a transaction due to an unknown error. It's frustrating and it happens to customers so often it has become commonplace.

In the worst case, the impact on the customer can be life-threatening. A bug in the UK's National Health Service software miscalculated 300,000 patients' risk levels of heart attacks. As a result, some patients were prescribed drugs with severe side effects, while others were told they were at low risk, resulting in otherwise preventable heart attacks and strokes.[9]

The impact can sometimes go beyond just the person using the software. For example, a bug in American Airlines' holiday scheduling software allowed all pilots to schedule time off during the Christmas holidays. This left over 15,000 flights without a pilot assigned to fly them. The result was not only a huge amount of stress for passengers trying to get home for Christmas but also for the families of the thousands of captains and copilots who had to cancel their vacation plans to return to work.[10] From a company's perspective, some of the effects of poor quality are public for all to see. With the American Airlines bug, there was potential loss of revenue from flight bookings, the overtime cost they incurred (as they paid 150% on top of normal salaries to get pilots to fly), and also the brand damage that came as the issue spread like wildfire over news outlets.

But a more damaging and often overlooked issue is how poor quality can affect the company internally. We've been inside organizations where QA was a disaster. Heads of development knew they had serious product quality issues but were constantly pushed to release. Software engineers constantly had to rework the codebase, stuck in an endless loop of fixing bugs instead of working on developing new features.

Who wants to work in that kind of environment where teams feel like they are on a forced death march, putting in overtime on a project destined to fail? That environment saps the energy, creativity, and motivation right out of the team. Managing in this environment can be a vicious cycle as you can lose your best team members and the remaining team can become even more frustrated and disillusioned.

People want to be part of creating great, game-changing products that help others, disrupt the status quo, or at least provide some sort of real value. Nobody wants to create an awful product.

Being a leader and seeing the press highlight issues in your software, while knowing you might be losing your best people internally, doesn't paint a great picture for your personal wellbeing or career.

When the CEO of subprime lender Provident Financial announced a software glitch that led to collecting only a little more than half of loan debts on time, the stock price tumbled 74% in a single day; he resigned shortly thereafter.[11]

In a report estimating the global cost of bad QA, one survey respondent said:

Every CIO I've ever known has had large, board [of directors]-visible projects where a defect discovered at the release date is so critical that it requires a major redesign of the project that leads to tens, if not hundreds of millions of dollars in costs, massive delays, and a huge loss of credibility.[12]

Imagine being in charge of a product or feature like that. Imagine being in a meeting with your boss or the chairman of the board, trying to explain to them how such a monumental design flaw got overlooked, despite the thousands of labor-hours in development and testing.

Poor quality can have a huge impact on your customers, your company, and your career. As leaders of quality, it's our responsibility to ensure we help guide our teams and colleagues in a direction that positively impacts the 3Cs.

LAYING THE FOUNDATIONS FOR LEADING QUALITY

When Mike Jones took over as CTO of uSwitch (then valued at $10.3 million), he took a deep dive into what the previous team had built...and almost wished he hadn't. [13]

Things were pretty bad.

uSwitch helped consumers compare and switch from one utility provider to another. As the company grew from a startup into a larger organization with nine distinct engineering teams, internal workflows had begun to break down. Product development efforts were diffused. Quality levels were not where Mike wanted them to be.

One of the first questions he posed to his new team was, "What business metric are we aiming to move?" No one knew.

As he told us, "People were too caught up in the process and not the outcome."

From building multiple businesses before, Mike knew that the best way to move teams forward was to have them all laser-focused on only one or two metrics.

His first step was to work out which metric would have the biggest impact on the company's growth. Since the company made revenue every time a customer used their platform to switch energy providers, he set the growth metric as "number of switches."

Focusing on more business-related KPIs was something product teams were used to, but this was a serious mind shift for the engineering and test teams. They weren't used to being measured like this and were unsure how to directly impact such a high-level metric. Mike, however, was relentless. Every build, feature, release, and issue was prioritized against the question, "What will make more users switch?"

As the teams' thinking changed to align with the "switches" metric, uSwitch began to see incredible growth. Over the next five years, they would grow from a $10.3-million business to being acquired for over $200 million.

As the CTO, Mike could have taken the traditional approach and focused solely on the engineering aspect of his role. Instead, he ensured that he and his team were also focused on creating the most business value and helping the customer get the most out of their product. With this focus, his team had clarity on what was important and how to align their efforts, resulting in a higher-quality product and a better experience for their end users.

As the number of customers who switched grew, so did the company. The engineering and quality teams involved in building the product could see how their work had a direct impact on helping the business grow to a company worth over $200 million. An improvement in all of the 3Cs.

In the past, software leaders looked at their roles solely through the lens of their technical function. Just as the TQM movement in manufacturing brought the focus of business outcomes and "providing value to the customer" to the forefront of executives' minds, today's software leaders are beginning to do the same.

As you begin to connect the work of your quality teams to business outcomes (a subject we'll explore more in Chapter 8), you'll start to see the effect on the 3Cs: happier customers who get the most value out of your software while dealing with fewer issues, a company whose core growth metric is continually growing, and the knowledge that you and your team were a major contributor to that success.

CHAPTER 1 SUMMARY (TL;DR)

- History has repeated itself: manufacturing first focused on optimization (speed) and then on customer value through quality; the same is happening in software development.

- Poor quality has a negative effect on the 3Cs: your customers, your company, and ultimately your career.

- You can look after your customers, company, and career by having a quality process that focuses on business outcomes and customer value.

2 | THE POWER OF A QUALITY NARRATIVE

"If you want to bring a fundamental change in people's belief and behavior...you need to create a community around them, where those new beliefs can be practiced and expressed and nurtured."

Malcolm Gladwell, *The Tipping Point: How Little Things Can Make a Big Difference*

One of the things that blocks leaders from being able to make the change they want in their organization is the organization's existing culture of quality.

Coming from a technical background myself, I used to have quite an aversion to words like "culture." At times, they seemed like terms used by business schools rather than having real-world implications. It's not uncommon for engineering leaders to feel this way. Jason Cohen, the founder and CTO of WP Engine, describes the moment he began to understand the importance of culture:

It made me think that there might be other attributes that contribute to the success of a company besides how many lines of code you could write in a day. It made me realize that, no matter what your position on this culture stuff was, you still had a culture at your company. If you're like I was, a skeptical, engineering-type founder, and say, "I don't care about all this touchy-feely stuff. It's all horseshit. All I care about are results and performance," even that is a statement of culture.[14]

You're saying that you value one thing above another.

However, even when you understand the importance of culture, it is still hard to make it tangible. When referring to the culture of quality inside a company, we've always found it easier to talk about it in terms of the "quality narrative."

A quality narrative is the way people think and talk about quality in a company, and just as Jason described, whether you know it or not, a narrative exists and it affects your company's culture around quality every day.

The clearer you understand the existing narrative, the easier it becomes for you to work out how you need to adjust the narrative to make the changes you want in your organization and achieve your goals.

Based on our observations and our conversations with different companies, there are three main types of narratives:

- **The Ownership Narrative** – discussions around who is responsible for quality
- **The "How to Test" Narrative** – discussions around what the right ways to test or what tools should be used to improve quality
- **The Value Narrative** – discussions around what the return on investment is for investing in quality

As leaders of quality inside our companies, it's important to be able to observe which narrative is holding us back from our goals so that we can address it. Let's dig a little deeper into each of them to find out more.

THE OWNERSHIP NARRATIVE

When describing the Ownership Narrative, we often say it's the foundational narrative. With a good Ownership Narrative in place, there is a higher focus on quality throughout the company and implementing changes to improve quality generates less friction.

When people talked about quality in the past, the Ownership Narrative was often focused around the test teams or the engineering teams being responsible for quality. But everyone in a company has a part to play; it's too important to be left to one team.

Let's take Snapchat, for example. In February 2017, the social media app faced pressure from an underwhelming IPO and had their backs up against the wall.[15] Growth was stalling. They had projected adding three times as many new users as they actually did.

The sluggish growth could be traced back to problems with their Android app. The reviews on the Google Play store were full of complaints about how buggy it was. Users on Reddit demanded answers as to why things were so bad.

From our experience and external perspective, the quality issues plaguing their Android app were not due to the work of the test team. Could they have been driven by a management decision? The previous year, CEO Evan Spiegel had directed his teams to prioritize their iOS app, believing it would generate greater revenue per user than Android. (Probably not the best strategic decision, given that Android accounted for 77% of mobile platforms, being used by 2.5 billion people globally.) In this same time period, Instagram capitalized on the void left in the market, capturing a huge group of Snapchat's dissatisfied customers.

Regardless of whether Snapchat's strategy ultimately turns out to be good or bad, the point is that management teams can affect software quality through the decisions they make, where they invest resources, and how they communicate internally.

As a piece of software goes from idea through to production, many different team members are directly involved in the quality of the product. Product managers make sure that the right thing is being built in the first place, designers ensure that the software is intuitive for an end user, engineers build the product, and the test teams work to support quality efforts throughout the process. But, outside of the path from idea to production, other teams also play a role in quality.

Take customer support, for example. David Cancel, former CPO of HubSpot, wrote in his book *HYPERGROWTH,*

At HubSpot, we'd have the support team, and we'd say, "Hey support, we want to fix the problems that you're seeing the most. We pledge to do that work, but you need to do the work of organizing and prioritizing what we should be focusing on." ...most of the support call-drivers end up being user experience issues.

As quality leaders inside our companies, we must not look at quality as a siloed responsibility of the test and engineering teams, but rather must widen the Ownership Narrative so that everyone understands their part in ensuring a high-quality product gets delivered. The best way to move the needle on a KPI that is impacted by multiple departments is to set up an autonomous, cross-functional team (which we'll refer to throughout this book as your quality team) to work on it. Recognizing the level of interdependence between teams to create a quality product is the essence of the Ownership Narrative.

Everybody affects quality. That's why improving quality has to encompass more than just testing tasks. It has to be an integral part of your organization's identity and culture.

THE "HOW TO TEST" NARRATIVE

The "How to Test" Narrative is the one the QA industry talks about the most. It's the sum of all the tactics, strategies, tools, and services that can be used to improve quality. This narrative can go wrong when one of two things happen.

First, when teams develop a "silver bullet" mentality, a sense that one particular type of testing or tool is all that's needed to improve quality. When we play chess, football, or the piano, there isn't just one way of doing it. There are multiple approaches.

The same is true when it comes to how to test. One size does not fit all. We commonly see companies over-relying on one type of testing, or bouncing from one idea to another in the hope that there is a magic fix for their quality issues. From all the companies that we've worked with and interviewed, we've seen that it's a blend of approaches that proves the most successful, because different types of testing (e.g., unit tests or exploratory tests) provide you with different types of information. It's all of those pieces of information that help you build a better-quality product.

The second problem is when the strategy of how to test is based on copying someone else's tactics without understanding why they did it or the unique situation the company was in (not to mention the problems or limitations they are now facing since implementing them).

If you asked ten engineers to build the same feature, you would likely get ten different approaches on how to build it. And with those variations, you may need to test it in different ways. Ideas on how to test that haven't taken into context the maturity of your team, infrastructure, or budget will probably have you heading in the wrong direction.

In *Your Strategy Needs a Strategy: How to Choose and Execute the Right Approach*, author Martin Reeves hits the nail on the head when he says,

"Strategy is, in essence, problem solving, and the best approach depends upon the specific problem at hand. Your environment dictates your approach to strategy."

There are different types of software products, different software development methodologies, and different user expectations and requirements. Without context, your "How to Test" Narrative could be flawed.

The best narratives on how to test focus on two things.

First, having a clear understanding of the different options and ways to test. Once you know this, you can assess the benefits, limitations, and type of information that each option provides. This will help you make better strategic decisions.

The second is a clear understanding of the maturity of your team, product, and company. This context ensures that the choices made fit with the current stage of development.

Over time, the maturity of your team, product, and company will evolve. This means the "How to Test" Narrative isn't static. It adapts as you change. In Chapter 5, we'll take a deeper dive into this concept as we discuss how quality changes with product maturity.

THE VALUE NARRATIVE

If the "How to Test" Narrative is the one the industry talks about the most, the Value Narrative is at the other end of the spectrum we don't discuss it enough. This narrative is about the value that focusing on quality brings to a company.

On the surface, most companies agree that quality and testing are important; however, when we dig deeper and start to listen to the internal conversations happening around investing in quality, it's interesting to hear who treats quality as an investment to be maximized versus a cost to be minimized. As Warren Buffett likes to say, "Only when the tide goes out do you discover who has been swimming naked."

All too often, management teams are not always convinced of the tangible value of investing in quality, until their company experiences quality issues like we saw with American Airlines' holiday scheduling bug in Chapter 1.

The methods to invest in quality are easy to understand and tangible, like new staff, infrastructure, tooling, and third-party vendors. However, it's not always easy to measure results like increased customer satisfaction, improved internal efficiency, and time saved by your team. This makes demonstrating the return on investment (ROI) hard.

When talking about the value that investing in quality brings, it's important to focus on three main areas: revenue potential, savings, and risk mitigation.

Revenue Potential

How can you demonstrate (or talk about) the work quality teams are doing in a way that highlights the missed revenue opportunity if quality is overlooked? Or the revenue potential from focusing on a particular aspect of quality? A few ways to do this could include:

Improving the company's core growth metric – As we will see in Chapter 8, having your quality teams focusing on the core metric that contributes toward company growth helps to keep everyone aligned. It also allows you to show a clearer correlation between the work the teams are doing and the contribution to the business, as we saw in the Indonesia story at the start of this book.

Describing how an increase in speed improves time to market – For example, if there has been an internal focus on developers unit testing before committing code, this frees up time for testers to focus on testing—not checking whether or not an engineer has met the acceptance criteria or being held up by a crashing bug or basic error that an engineer should have picked up through their own "happy path" testing. This ultimately results in the build achieving release-level quality faster, which means fewer build revisions and testing cycles within a sprint. However, when communicated, this should be discussed in terms of its ability to improve the company's time to market.

Uncovering additional value for the customer – In addition to quality teams focusing on the company's growth metric, they need to pay close attention to the value that the customer gets from the product (covering onboarding, engagement, and retention). This way, they can increase the likelihood of the customer using your product and paying for it in the future.

Savings

When we talk about the work we do, do we speak in terms of the financial savings that we are able to make or influence in the company? For example, consider the following:

Monetary value of your team's time – Investing in quality can help maximize the productivity of both your engineering and internal test teams. That might be due to your engineers no longer having to context-switch, deal with reworking features, or do an additional sprint before the feature is ready. It could be that your internal testing team don't have to focus on executing test cases better performed by an automated process or crowd. Regardless, the monetary saving from investing in quality can be seen in the hours that a person saves in a day, which can be used elsewhere.

Saving on infrastructure costs – There are also more direct monetary savings that can be achieved with things like infrastructure costs. Take, for example, the need to buy new devices for testing on. This cost can be reduced by utilizing crowd-testing services or device farms. Not only does this save on the capital expenditure of having to buy such devices, it also reduces the need to maintain and upgrade them over time.

Risk Mitigation

The risk of having a critical issue arrive in production is often one of the primary reasons that management increases the budget to invest in quality. No one wants a PR disaster on their hands from a lack of testing.

When I hear people talking about the value of quality, these conversations often center on risk mitigation, sometimes touching on the savings that could be made, but unfortunately, revenue potential is rarely highlighted.

Understanding how to talk about quality by starting with its revenue potential and then discussing savings and risk mitigation is an important step to having people look at quality teams not as a cost center, but as an asset that can help contribute to company growth.

UNCOVERING YOUR QUALITY NARRATIVE

Information about what your quality narrative is can be seen all around you in staff members' actions and attitudes regarding quality. Many execs we speak to have a sense of where the biggest problem areas are. However, to confirm your assumptions, you can use a simple technique to understand the current narrative in your company.

Ask different members of your company, "What are the top three comments you hear about quality around the business?" The key here is to ask them what they hear. You will often get an unfiltered response based on how they feel about quality.

Once you understand the existing quality narrative, you can start thinking about where you want it to be. How do you want quality to be perceived internally and externally? Where do you want your team to be in twelve months? Examples could include "Everyone in the company feels responsible for the quality of the product" or "We are investing in improving the quality of our products from a people, process, and technology perspective." These initial statements become the foundation for knowing what change you need to make to move toward your ideal narrative.

CHAPTER 2 SUMMARY (TL;DR)

- Your company's culture of quality exists as a quality narrative whether you intentionally state it or not.
- There are three main types of quality narratives that exist inside companies:
    - **The Ownership Narrative** – who is responsible for quality
    - **The "How to Test" Narrative** – what the right ways are to test or what tools should be used to improve quality
    - **The Value Narrative** – what the return on investment is from investing in quality
- Understanding your quality narrative is the first step toward shifting the culture of quality within your organization.

WANT HELP WORKING OUT YOUR QUALITY NARRATIVE??

You can download our worksheet at:

lqbook.co/resources

3 | LEADING A CULTURE OF QUALITY

"Leadership is essentially a task of persuasion—
of winning people's minds and hearts."
Stephen Denning, *The Leader's Guide to Storytelling:*
Mastering the Art and Discipline of Business Narrative

When Arylee McSweaney accepted a new role at Etsy as Senior Manager of Test Engineering Strategy, she was tasked with changing the engineering culture to incorporate more test automation and improve QA standards.

One of the first areas she wanted to focus on was increasing the ownership of quality across the business by motivating engineering teams to budget time into their development sprints to write tests.[16] She soon realized that the reason they weren't writing the tests wasn't because they didn't think it was important. There simply wasn't enough time to account for writing tests in the middle of development sprints. They faced the tradeoff between writing tests and dealing with aggressive release deadlines. The deadlines were winning, despite the complications it could create down the line.

Arylee could have gone about changing their thinking by challenging them head-on. Instead, she decided to go about it in a smart way. She started with a survey, asking engineers for their input and ideas around quality improvement. One significant insight from the results was that the engineers wanted better mechanisms for voicing their wins, challenges, and failures, especially around automation.

She created Etsy's first "lightning talk" series, known across the organization as "TEST Etsy." These were quarterly events where engineers at any level could voice their ideas and frustrations, with attendees often including their fellow engineers, managers, and even the CTO.

The personal stories they shared resonated with everyone, giving the engineers personal validation regarding their challenges, from their peers as well as their managers. Beyond that, it helped leadership better understand their situation and the reality of their workload. And vice versa: it helped shift the engineers' perception of quality to better understand leadership's priorities.

When the engineers made quality a higher priority, doing things like budgeting time for writing test scripts during development came naturally. She supported this change in thinking by circulating a weekly TEST report whereby each engineering group could measure their performance against others'. Progress soared across the board. Soon after, allocating time for testing-related tasks became an integral part of their software development lifecycle (and remains so to this day).

Arylee isn't alone in having to use her influence and persuasion skills to drive change. As leaders, we often invest hours of time doing some form of non-sales selling. Daniel Pink, author of *To Sell Is Human*, found that people who are in non-sales-based roles spend nearly 40% of their time (roughly twenty-four minutes of every hour) engaged in some form of persuading, influencing, or convincing others.

There are four major areas to master in order to influence your quality narrative and adjust the culture of quality within your company:

- **Knowing the audience you need to influence** and what their motivations, goals and fears are
- **Creating empathy to increase alignment and understanding** between teams and individuals
- **Supporting the narrative with evidence** to add weight to your ideas
- **Cultivating internal champions** to help create momentum

The best leaders use the above methods to get everyone around them on board with the changes they want to make.

KNOW THE AUDIENCE YOU NEED TO INFLUENCE

The first step in moving toward your ideal quality narrative is to know the audience you need to influence. In most situations, there is normally more than one person that you'll need to persuade to get buy-in to your ideas. Start by writing down a list of all of these people, from your boss to your peers or even people in another manager's team.

Next, consider these questions for each person:

- What are their goals and objectives?
- What concerns/challenges do they face in their day-to day-role?
- Why would they object to your idea?
- How does your idea impact them and their teams?

Once you've answered these questions, you'll notice how different the motivations are for each of the people you've listed. Use this as a basis to find a way to speak the language of the person you're trying to influence. Find what's important to them, and then frame the issue in terms that make them sit up and take notice.

Instead of talking about features and information, highlight the benefits your idea can deliver, especially as it relates to their worries and wants. Paint a picture of the future: what will it provide them with that they don't have now?

At a recent CIO Panel, former CIO of Shared Services at Procter & Gamble, Andy Walter said that, when speaking to senior management, you need to "raise the discussion" and answer a basic question for them: "What can I do with my business, now that I have this, that I couldn't do before?"

This means that, when speaking with a management audience, you should focus the discussion around customers and the effects on the business.

Shesh Patel, Engineering Manager at *The New York Times*, understands this principle perfectly. He adapts how he presents his ideas based on the person or people he is speaking to.[17] For example, when he wanted to implement a new project that would reduce the time it took to run regression tests, he adapted how he explained it to different people.

When speaking with the leadership team, he focused on the number of dollars saved by implementing the idea, as well as what could be done with the savings to further improve the team's ability to release high-quality products. When communicating with the product team, he highlighted how it would improve the whole team's ability to release new features quicker. Likewise, while talking with the engineers, he underscored how it would affect the engineers experience, emphasizing everything from how it would make their release process easier, to the reduction in the number of flaky tests they would have to deal with a point he knew was a major frustration for the team at the time.

One idea, three different ways of aligning it with individual goals.

By knowing more about the person you want to influence, you can ensure that the way you communicate appeals to them. By tailoring your message this way, more people will buy into your ideas, as they will have a clearer understanding of what's in it for them.

CREATE EMPATHY TO INCREASE ALIGNMENT AND UNDERSTANDING

When a car's wheels are out of alignment, steering becomes harder. Your tires begin to wear unevenly, causing a subtle drag on the car. Your fuel efficiency drops. It becomes dangerous to move at high speeds and, in extreme cases, it can even lead to an accident.

The same is true for misalignment in your company.

But achieving alignment is hard. How can you help people with diverse viewpoints and responsibilities to better understand the reality and mentality of their counterparts? Each team has a different perspective on quality. They all think and talk about it differently.

To paraphrase the classic quote from *To Kill a Mockingbird*, you never really get to know a person until you walk around in their shoes. Empathy is the ability to understand and share the feelings of someone else. When team members better understand the work that goes into each other's role, they have more context to understand how to work together.

In an effort to solve this dilemma, you might try an approach adopted by Ben Horowitz (the venture capitalist behind Zynga, Twitter, and Stack Overflow): what he calls the *Freaky Friday* Management Technique. After watching the famous body-swap film, he decided to switch two of his executives whose departments had "[gone] to war with each other."[18] The Head of Sales became the Head of Customer Support and vice versa. He called the result "miraculous." Horowitz said:

From that day to the day we sold the company, the sales engineering and support organizations worked better together than any other major groups in the company, all thanks to Freaky Friday, perhaps the most insightful management training film ever made.

What really happened here was an increase in empathy and understanding of each other's role. This created a shared perspective on how to reach an end goal. When it comes to applying this kind of thinking inside teams, you could use a less extreme approach, such as cross-functional pairing sessions.

These pairing sessions are designed to have people from different disciplines work together to share ideas and avoid misalignment later down the line.

At social network Xing, Senior Product Designer Nikkel Blaase pairs his designers with developers "so that we can easily discuss layouts and technical restrictions, or can make fast decisions. Communication is a key factor when it comes to collaboration with developers."[19] Pivotal Labs take it one step further by having their developers and designers pair together for half a day to fix design tweaks, an otherwise frustrating task to do via their internal chat system. This kind of activity saves time and builds empathy between departments.[20]

Atlassian, the makers of software products like Jira and Confluence, have a great way of pairing the developers with their quality teams. The quality function focus on "quality assistance" wherein they show the engineers how to get better at testing their own code, especially with exploratory testing techniques.[21] Armed with that, the engineers can think through scenarios more clearly and spot their own bugs before the code leaves their desk.

In other cases, like in Arylee's example, the empathy isn't targeted between teams but between management and those in more operational roles. In these situations, increasing the visibility of what teams do on a day-to-day basis through "lunch and learns" or lightning talks can encourage more open communication about challenges and successes. Management can also go one step further and spend time sitting with the team to understand what they are actually doing.

SUPPORT THE NARRATIVE WITH EVIDENCE

You can use different forms of evidence to support your quality narrative. Some forms of evidence will be internal, utilizing information and data that already exist or creating small experiments with internal teams. Other forms of evidence may be external, utilizing information outside of your company.

Internal Evidence

Having internal evidence that your idea is worth pursuing has the huge advantage of being relatable to the people inside your company. This increases the level of empathy available when aiming to create change.

Arylee used internal surveys to gather information on what the team cared about, giving her useful evidence based on the engineering team's feelings around quality. An alternative approach is to perform a small internal experiment to prove the merit of your idea.

In the early days of Airbnb, code was hitting the production servers without many checks and this was becoming problematic as the company scaled. Lou Kosak, one of the engineers at the time, started a small internal experiment to see how they could change the way his team, and others, worked. He wrote the following in a blog post:[22]

Eventually, a few people...started submitting pull requests for their changes. This was never introduced as a mandatory policy; we never disabled pushing to master or shamed people for doing so. But as those few, then a team, then several teams started doing this...it became clear that this process of peer review led to less bad code hitting production, and therefore fewer outages.

With the success of the experiment, Lou and the rest of his engineering team ensured that all new hires were briefed on best practices that involved submitting pull requests. This naturally led to everyone adopting the same practices over time.

Shortly after, the engineers decided to include writing tests with any new code, while also beginning to educate teams about the importance of testing: they spoke at meetups, held "office hours" and shared recommended readings to increase their teams' knowledge. New hires were also made into champions of testing, while further investment was made into the testing infrastructure, making it easier to write and run tests.

By gathering evidence in a small way, Lou and his team were able to influence the whole testing process.

External Evidence

If you don't have internal evidence, you can also use external evidence. However, the effect of external evidence is different. Rather than adding empathy, it is used to increase credibility, illustrating that your ideas are proven and have a high chance of being successful. There are many different sources you can use: data from industry studies, presentations from talks, or even books (like this one) that have examples from well-known companies.

When using external evidence, make sure you have a good understanding of what the statistics really mean or why the example worked. Otherwise you could end up falling into the "How to Test" Narrative mistake we discussed in Chapter 2 where there isn't enough understanding of how it needs to be adapted to your current situation.

CULTIVATE INTERNAL CHAMPIONS

Groupthink, consensus, or social proof—no matter what you call it, there is influence in having others around you who share the same ideas as you.[23]

To lead change, you will need help, whether it comes from your boss, your peers, or people who report to you. Your allies don't necessarily need to be in the development or quality teams.

Discover executives and other key stakeholders who might be receptive to your ideas and focus on fostering a relationship there. You might need to follow Lou's example at Airbnb and start a grassroots effort to find like-minded professionals, people who believe that quality is at the heart of software success. Anyone in your organization who sees the importance of making quality a higher priority is a potential ally... and the more you work to lead the effort at establishing a better quality narrative, the more these types of potential allies and champions will make themselves known.

When it comes to promoting ideas around quality, the Atlassian quality team focuses on sharing QA best practices, enhancing product/feature quality, and improving development-QA workflows. Spotify have a similar role with a slightly different job description: their "Quality Advocates" are tasked with promoting the importance of quality itself within the company.

Once you've begun gathering your internal champions, if you're lucky, you may even one day echo the words that Lou from Airbnb put at the start of his blog post: "I'd like to share with you how we...changed our culture to make testing a first-class citizen."

By focusing on developing your skills around influence and persuasion, you'll be able to forge a stronger culture around quality within your company.

CHAPTER 3 SUMMARY (TL;DR)

- In order to lead quality inside your company, you must become a student of persuasion and influence.
- Ways to improve your influence include:
    - **Knowing the audience you need to influence** and what their motivations, goals and fears are
    - **Creating empathy to increase alignment and understanding** between teams and individuals
    - **Supporting the narrative with evidence** to add weight to your ideas
    - **Cultivating internal champions** to help create momentum

SECTION II

MASTERING YOUR STRATEGIC
QUALITY DECISIONS

4 | FOUNDATIONS: MANUAL TESTING VS. AUTOMATION

"The first rule of any technology used in a business is that automation applied to an efficient operation will magnify the efficiency. The second is that automation applied to an inefficient operation will magnify the inefficiency."

Bill Gates

Mark was in the conference room for the team's morning stand-up. The company had just hired a new VP of Engineering a couple of weeks before. On this particular day, the VP was explaining his thoughts on the direction of the team. His main priority was to increase development velocity. A big part of his vision was to reduce the QA bottleneck by automating 100% of testing with a new automation framework.[24]

"I believe we've found a platform that can help us automate all of our testing and shore up our quality issues," he remarked.

Mark was skeptical, however. The new VP wasn't around the year before when the company had first tried to move toward automation.

At that time, there was a sense of urgency. It seemed like everybody else was automating and they certainly didn't want to be left behind. It sounded great in theory.

In reality, it was chaos.

They'd argued about what to automate: Should they focus on new features or begin with legacy parts of the system? Who was going to be in charge of maintaining the tests? Engineers or testers?

During this initial attempt, automation didn't speed up delivery. In fact, they got so far behind that, just to ship the next release, they had to suspend all automation-related tasks to make their delivery date. After that, they never picked it back up. Worse, no one ever talked about it. It was like a failed experiment everyone was too ashamed to remember.

Mark looked around the meeting room and saw that many of his coworkers were thinking the same thing. One by one, they started voicing their concerns, but the new VP was having none of it. So, they all put their heads down and went to work.

The ensuing months of implementation were even worse than their first attempt at automation.

- They over-optimized parts of their testing infrastructure.
- Some parts of the application were changing too quickly for automation to be viable.
- Their testing infrastructure kept breaking.
- They spent far too much time trying to make all the different testing tools work together.
- Usability suffered as more and more bugs slipped through the cracks.

Customers began to take notice. Then they began to complain. Then they began to abandon the app altogether. At first, it was just a few, but then even some of their most faithful customers left them for the competition. Management couldn't ignore the problem anymore. They directed the engineering teams to forget automation and do whatever it took to keep their remaining customers. They did bring quality back up, but by then, the damage had already been done.

A year or so later, Mark had taken a great job at another company. When he came in, he found them in the middle of automating their testing. He said to himself, "Oh, great. Here we go again."

But, to his surprise, automation was working. Contrasting the two experiences, Mark pointed to four key differences:

1. **Team culture:** They had a cohesive team approach to problem-solving and process improvement.
2. **Expectations:** They didn't envision automation being the magic answer to all their problems; they set their expectations appropriately for what it could deliver as well as its limitations.
3. **Timing:** They knew what tools were appropriate based on the product's maturity and lifecycle.
4. **Infrastructure:** They had the correct infrastructure in place to allow them to get the most out of their automation efforts.

Automation has its time and place. However, for some reason, many believe in a fantasy version of its possibilities. Why has a whole industry bought into the idea of full automation when only 14% of enterprise software is currently automated?[25]

Just like in *The Wizard of Oz*, to get to the truth we first need to understand who's behind the curtain.

BEHIND THE CURTAIN OF AUTOMATION

Edward Bernays was the nephew of Dr. Sigmund Freud and is considered "the father of public relations."[26] He was named one of the one hundred most influential Americans of the twentieth century[27] because he heavily influenced business, politics, and even national culture.

Bernays' line of thinking eventually led to what we know today as behavioral economics and consumer choice. Or, simply put, why and how people buy. What he discovered was that to influence people on a massive scale (say, influencing an entire industry to believe that one particular approach is the absolute best approach), you need "choice architects." These are the people who steer the message the way they want it to go.

When we looked at the choice architects that created the misconceptions of automated testing, we came across something completely unexpected. It was us: testing professionals.

Facing increased competition, testing vendors' marketing teams pushed the limits when they described what was possible with their tools. Their sales teams would boast about their customers' successes with automation, leaving out the gory details. When implementations did go wrong, it was put down as "poor execution," rather than a problem with the tool. Instead of critically evaluating those "successes," we bought into the hype.

Selling the dreams of automation is one part of the equation. Let's dig into the other part: the three drivers behind why companies were (and remain) so desperate to buy into the hype.

First and foremost, they needed an answer to their primary problem of speed. Teams face incredible levels of competition to get their products out as quickly as possible. If you can automate six minutes' worth of tasks a day for a team of ten people, that's an extra hour of a person's time every day. Not to mention that the kinds of things that can be automated are often repetitive tasks. The time saved could be invested in other high-value activities, such as exploratory testing, working more closely with teams to create a culture of quality, and thinking strategically about how quality can be improved for their products.

Second, automation is marketed as a way to perform more testing (i.e., scale) with the same resources. For teams constrained by budget and resources, it was seen as a way to expand their capabilities at a fraction of the costs, financially and time-wise.

Third, it was a way to maintain consistency. Computers execute the exact same test the exact same way, every single time. You never have to worry about missing or skipping something. It reduces the chances of introducing a bug into the process of testing itself and has a repeatable outcome.

But, like everything, automation has a price. A large amount of work goes into planning, preparing, executing, and maintaining sustainable automation efforts. That's in addition to all the work you're already doing in app development.

So, when should you use automation and when should you keep it manual?

CAN YOU AUTOMATE EVERYTHING?

While waiting to board a plane at London Heathrow, I read an article about the role of QA in DevOps by Dan Ashby,[28] then the Head of Testing at eBay. After reading it, I immediately sent an excited message to our well-connected friend, Vernon Richards: "Hey Vernon, I just read an article that captures what we've been debating around 'when to automate.' Do you happen to know a guy named Dan Ashby?"

He messaged back a second later: "Yeah, I'm sitting in front of him right now."

What were the odds!?

Vernon made the introduction and I was on a video call with Dan later that week. He walked me through his framework for recognizing when to use different types of testing. On the surface, it was a simple model, but it was that simplicity that made it so profound. His model has now become a cornerstone of our approach to testing.[29]

On his screenshare, Dan drew a box and labeled it "Information."

INFORMATION

Like a professor lecturing an eager student, he explained:

The majority of the work we do in testing is a continuous attempt to uncover information about things we're unaware of and to ensure that the things we think we know are still true. Once we have that information, we can then make a decision about what to do next.

He drew another box and wrote "Investigating," then drew yet another box, labeling it "Verifying."

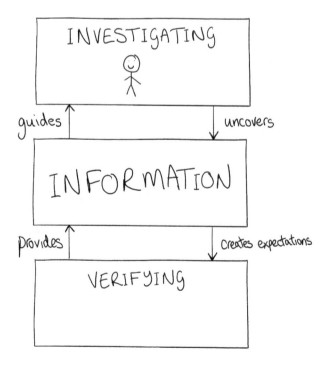

Dan continued:

So, when we think about testing, there are two broad types of testing we can do. The most common form is investigating. This is when we use our own creativity to uncover new information about a product. Every investigative activity gives you more information about the product. The more information you have, the more you can use it to guide further exploration. The amount of exploratory testing you can do is limited only by your imagination.

Pointing to the "Verifying" box, he said:

In these activities, you already have an expectation of what should happen. You simply want to check that it's still true. These are generally pass/fail situations. As long as the test goes as expected, you've verified that X is still true. If it fails, then you've uncovered a problem.

The problem with verifying activities is that you can only verify what you know needs to be checked. But once a problem is uncovered, you then have to investigate it. And that is why you will always need some form of manual testing.

When engineers create software, they can create a checklist of all the things it should do. An automation engineer can turn that checklist into a program to verify that, yes, this software does everything it's supposed to. However, there is a level of creativity required to identify ways in which the software wouldn't work, scenarios under which it might not perform as expected.

There will always be unexpected factors that need to be explored. It's hard to plan for the unknown. If you can't plan for it, you can't create an automation script for it. The result: you will always need specialized testers who can use human imagination, knowledge, and experience to do investigative forms of testing.

You can't automate creativity.

SHOULD YOU AUTOMATE EVERYTHING?

Once Dan had delivered those insights, I thought that was the end of the lesson. But like the sage he is, the lesson went a layer deeper.

Dan drew a line through the middle of the "Verifying" box. To the left of the line, he drew a stickman with a smiley face. To the right, he wrote a string of binary ones and zeros.

"Verifying activities can be done either by manual testing or via automated testing. The trick is to know when to apply which."

IBM conducted a study to answer this question. In a paper titled "Reducing the Cost of IT Operations Is Automation Always the Answer?"[30] the researchers calculated the costs of performing different tests manually versus automating. Their aim was to figure out the optimal point to automate a test case. They concluded that there were three main factors that led to automation being more efficient than manual testing:

1. The automated test case is expected to have a relatively long life without needing to be changed or edited.
2. The test case is comparatively easy to automate, i.e., it can be created from a generalized manual process; the more complex the task, the

more difficult it is to automate.

3. The comparative cost of automating is lower than that of executing the test manually.

When these three factors are in place, you can enjoy the benefits of automation: it scales, it provides faster feedback loops to developers when there is a problem, and it improves the accuracy of repetitive tasks.

Dan helped us realize that people are approaching the whole automation question wrong. Don't ask, "Should we automate or not?" Automation is just one way to test, a single tool in your toolkit. That's like asking an engineer, "What's the best way to code?" or asking a chef, "What's the best cooking method?" There are plenty of ways to code and cook; a professional wouldn't limit themselves to just one way every single time.

You have to realize that there are really two types of information-gathering activities in testing: investigating and verifying. Dan's framework showed us that using manual or automation doesn't have to be a binary choice. Manual by itself won't allow you to scale. Going 100% automated is impractical and, ultimately, unsustainable. The middle way is a blend between the two. It is fruitless to argue for or against either, much like arguing whether hammers or spanners are better.

The best tool depends on what you're trying to do.

CHAPTER 4 SUMMARY (TL;DR)

- Automating all your testing isn't a silver bullet and can be counter-productive if implemented in the wrong way.
- The question "Can we automate everything?" can be answered by looking at the two main types of testing activities:
  - **Investigating** activities require a human to uncover new information
  - **Verifying** activities confirm whether the information you expect is true or not and can be performed by a human or a machine
- To answer the question "Should you automate everything?" there are three factors that you should consider:
  - Length of time for which the automated test is expected to be used (the longer, the better)
  - The comparative ease of automating the task or process
  - The comparative cost of automating being less than that of executing the test manually

5 | HOW QUALITY CHANGES WITH PRODUCT MATURITY

"To create a product that incorporates customer feedback on early product increment, to release software in response to the latest market development, and to bring new functionality to the market quickly is only possible if the product exhibits the right quality."

Roman Pichler, author and product management expert

Through Global App Testing, Owais and I have had ringside seats, watching as our long-time clients have grown from fledgling startups to established companies, and to see others grow from regional businesses to having a global footprint.

As we watched their growth, we witnessed the changes in their customer bases in line with the five stages of technology adoption:[31]

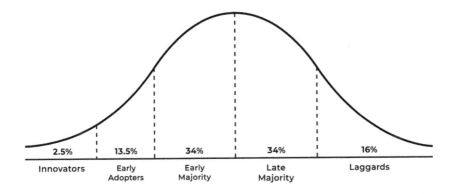

In the early 2000s, social media was still relatively new. We had services like Myspace and Bebo, but these were far from mainstream. Most people on social networks at the time were the innovators and early adopters of technology.

Over the subsequent years, more people have adopted social media. With the increase in adoption, the demographic of who uses each platform has expanded.[33] While many of the social media services started out with a younger audience, they have now grown to include the older generations of parents and grandparents. These people would be classified as the 'late majority' and 'laggards'. Each company must then adapt their product and view on quality to suit this new type of user.

Reflecting on our clients' product evolution as they grew, we noticed that the way their teams looked at testing also changed. Each product moved through three broad categories:

- **Validation:** product-market fit
- **Predictability:** creating a stable infrastructure for scale
- **Scaling:** minimizing negative impact to unlock growth

Those with user bases composed mostly of innovators and early adopters are in the validation stage. Users are often tech-savvy, enthusiastic about a new product, and somewhat forgiving as the product rapidly iterates through new versions. Product development focuses on a minimal viable product; it just has to be good enough to get feedback and iterate. The accompanying QA strategy is fairly ad hoc.

But when that user base grows to include the early majority, we move into the predictability stage, where the product will have a new set of development and QA priorities. As the product team finds its footing and the application begins to get more complicated, you find your team needing more reliability in your technology; you value stability more than you had during the validation stage and, accordingly, want your QA strategy to focus on allowing the team to move fast with the correct infrastructure.

Finally, once you begin to mature in your primary market, you may start to eye additional markets or opportunities, which, in turn, bring further demands. With an increase in late-majority users and laggards, you need a QA strategy that can help the company as it delivers scalable growth. We call this the scaling stage.

As a product evolves through these stages, your QA strategy will naturally change. Therefore, so too will the tactics and tools you use.

When things begin to break, it's not necessarily a sign that your QA has begun to fail. It could just indicate that your needs have changed and so you need to change your strategy to succeed.

THE VALIDATION STAGE: PRODUCT-MARKET FIT

When we first met Dominic Assirati, VP of Production Services at King, the company was already well established as the makers behind global phenomenon Candy Crush. They had developed more than 200 games, with a staggering 272 million monthly active users across their portfolio.[33] Dominic is in charge of making sure games get delivered to the right level of quality. Part of King's success has come from recognizing the three different stages of product maturity and having an appropriate testing strategy for each.

In the early part of a game's life, they don't know whether it'll be a hit or not. They assemble a small team to begin building it and track lots of metrics benchmarking it against how they know a successful game should perform in its early days. They want to make sure they are building something that customers want. In this environment, things are rapidly changing, so the way they think of QA and testing needs to stay flexible.[34]

Typically, resources and budget are severely constrained (even in a large company like King, various proof points need to be hit before they will commit substantial resources to a concept), and teams tend to stay as lean as possible. There's also a focus on unit testing, good communication to ensure solid code reviews, smooth build pipelines, and internal dogfooding.[35]

At this stage, automation isn't a primary focus. As Dominic puts it, "If you want to do it well, then you have to be prepared to invest long-term. It's not a fire-and-forget type of thing." It's not worth the time and effort to invest in automation until the product is out of this initial proof-of-concept phase.

Although the initial users of the product tend to be early adopters, who are a little more forgiving of issues, the quality level the product needs to be at is heavily dependent on customer expectations. The more mature the industry, the higher the expectations usually are.

In the early days of online dating, the experience itself was so novel that early adopters didn't have preconceived expectations of quality. Today, those same users aren't so forgiving with a newly launched dating service. From the first time they log in, they're already expecting to have an experience at least as good as Match.com or Tinder. They have an internal benchmark.

The bar is even higher for B2B products, especially in mature industries like banking and insurance. Developing an app in an environment like that necessitates moving slower and keeping quality higher before release, despite being in the validation stage.

During this stage, many features are often abandoned as the team quickly pivots and iterates. They're continually changing their business decisions around what should be built. It's hard to build a solid testing infrastructure because of the constant change and uncertainty. All of this leads to increasing complexity in the source code, leaving it more prone to bugs and other issues.

Because of how new the product is, manual testing activities allow you to remain more flexible than if you were to double down on test automation, which might not provide the best ROI at this stage. Your testing approach should focus on core user flows, new functionality, and unblocking critical user issues.

Some teams use beta users to support finding early issues. Unfortunately, you can only glean so much from non-professional feedback, because your real-world users aren't accustomed to providing structured feedback and relevant information, such as screenshots, videos, crash logs, and steps to reproduce. It can become a painstaking process to coordinate and work with them.

Companies like iHeartMedia (a US-based radio station with over 120 million users) utilize beta users to gather high-level feedback and then send that feedback to a crowd of professional testers to perform exploratory testing and test-case execution to identify the exact issue.

The core theme of this stage is cost-effectiveness and flexibility. It doesn't make sense to commit large-scale resources to an unproven idea. You will be in a continual state of flux while you iterate through challenges and opportunities until you either find a promising prototype or abandon the product altogether.

THE PREDICTABILITY STAGE: CREATING A STABLE INFRASTRUCTURE FOR SCALE

At the validation stage of a product, you're constantly iterating. But once you find product-market fit, your priorities shift from prototyping to supporting the core features.

You want, in a word, predictability.

At this stage, teams typically focus on software stability. Testing efforts revolve around tasks such as exploratory testing and writing test cases and automation scripts for stable features. With a viable product and market, it makes sense to put more resources behind the app and invest in testing infrastructure (e.g., optimizing code for testing, creating or expanding an automation suite, and creating tools to support quality).

Steve Janaway is VP of Engineering at Bloom & Wild, one of the fastest-growing tech companies in the UK. He describes the benefits of focusing on predictability at this stage:

...it makes the team, as a delivery unit, easier to predict and therefore easier to manage...the team is not being sidetracked with a bunch of live issues stemming from edge cases that nobody considered.

For Dominic and his team at King, once they reach this stage, one of the first issues they deal with is the technical debt that accrued during the validation stage. In a rush to find product-market fit, inevitably a team has taken shortcuts. They make it work and worry about doing it right later. (If there is a later.)

Like any debt, the longer you ignore it, the more it's going to hurt when you're finally forced to pay it off. But knowing this doesn't help with the pressure. Dominic describes the feeling of having a binary choice, with neither of the two options seeming favorable: "Should we invest the next three to five months embedding a test automation framework? Or should we focus on hitting the next major milestone for the lifecycle of that game?"

To deal with this delicate balance, King use a mixture of different tools and strategies. The team refactors the most important parts of their codebase as they begin to add new features.

They also increase the levels of automation on the game (which increases predictability) as well as utilizing a crowd of testers, both internally and through an external crowdsourced testing partner to support with regression testing. By using both, they ensure they have testing coverage as their automation is being developed out. Over time, they are able to prioritize which tests should be automated and which should run via the crowd.

At the predictability stage, it's clear that the extreme choices, to either continue moving forward without a solid testing foundation or to stop everything and write all of the missing automated tests, are both unacceptable. The move to a more automated platform becomes the goal. But getting there isn't done overnight.

You want to find tactics that incrementally move things forward, balancing the short-term benefits against the long-term costs.

THE SCALING STAGE: MINIMIZING NEGATIVE IMPACT TO UNLOCK GROWTH

By the time a King game has a substantial amount of user growth, the development and quality teams support the game on every major device/OS combination and in most locations across the world. At this stage, the focus is on accelerating growth through new user adoption and increased engagement for existing users. The trouble with performing at this scale is that even a "small" problem can affect a high number of people.

In the validation stage, a bug that affects 1% of users isn't even on the quality team's radar. In the predictability stage, that small of a percentage is a low-priority edge case. But once you're in the scaling stage, 1% of your users may comprise more people than your entire user base in the first two stages.

A tiny bug affecting just a single percent of Google Maps users amounts to over ten million people.[36] That's roughly the equivalent of Portugal or Sweden not being able to use Google Maps.

The more your business is connected to an application, the higher the stakes. Tech-first organizations like Uber are completely reliant on their app or website. A bug affecting Uber's UK users for even an hour would result in real, immediate financial loss.

For companies like Starbucks, whose application is not their main business, there isn't a direct financial implication, but a bug can still tarnish their brand. If the Starbucks app crashes for a couple of hours, they can still make coffee. However, the company loses credibility because its brand is tied to the performance of all of its branded assets.

When something like that happens, the media is quick to make headlines out of it. In August 2012, financial services firm Knight Capital lost an estimated $440 million in thirty minutes due to a software bug in their trading platform that flooded the market with unintended trades. Within two days, the firm's shares lost 75% of their value.[37]

During this stage of growth, companies usually use a wide blend of testing types. For King, they use this period to go deeper into performance testing, looking at battery, network, and CPU consumption to ensure the app is truly meeting customer expectations.

The last thing for us to consider when discussing how quality changes with product maturity is how to deal with legacy software.

Working with Legacy Software

If your team didn't implement the right testing foundations, such as the unit tests and integration tests described in the validation and predictability stages, the team will be unaware of the existing dependencies in the codebase. A small change made in one area might introduce new bugs in seemingly unrelated areas. Compounding the problem is the fact that by this time, so many people have been working on the codebase (many of whom are no longer working on the project) that it's impossible to understand the dependencies between everything.

If you find your team in this situation, we recommend reading Michael Feathers' book *Working Effectively with Legacy Code*. In it, he outlines this five-step method:

1. Identify where in the codebase you need to make changes.
2. Find the right test points.
3. Break those dependencies into smaller modules.
4. Write the tests.
5. Make changes and refactor.

As your product grows in complexity and user adoption, the challenges around quality change. There may not be one method of how to test at each stage, but there are common challenges that need to be overcome. You will always need a blend of different testing types, and that blend should evolve to match your product's stage of maturity.

It's more work than the silver-bullet answer so many people want, but adopting a context-specific approach to testing—and constantly adapting it to that ever-changing context—*is* the real answer to the question, "What should my testing strategy be?"

CHAPTER 5 SUMMARY (TL;DR)

- Over a product's lifecycle, its users will evolve from innovators to early adopters through late majority and laggards.
- As you move through the product's lifecycle, there are three broad categories where your approach to QA will change:
    - **Validation:** product-market fit
    - **Predictability:** creating a stable infrastructure for scale
    - **Scaling:** minimizing negative impact to unlock growth
- When things begin to break, it's not necessarily a sign that your QA has begun to fail. It could just indicate that your needs have changed and so you need to change your strategy to suit.

6|IMPROVING FEEDBACK LOOPS TO SUPERCHARGE CONTINUOUS TESTING

"There is always space for improvement, no matter how long
you've been in the business."
Oscar De La Hoya, professional boxer and Olympic gold medalist

Ashley Hunsberger is the Director of Release Engineering at Blackboard, an educational technology company. Their learning management system has over a hundred million users across 17,000 schools and organizations, including 75% of US colleges and universities. With their level of reach, ensuring that they have a quality product is crucial to them. [38]

Over her fourteen years with the company, she's experienced the multiyear transition of a team working in a waterfall methodology, then moving to Agile and DevOps practices. As her team shifted to a continuous deployment model, they began creating an extensive automation suite. As the product development efforts became more and more sophisticated, she began to realize that QA wasn't keeping up. As efficient as the tests were, the results could take five or six hours, meaning that they had to run them overnight. They couldn't get information that their engineers could act on until the following morning, at the earliest—still too slow to keep up with the pace of development.

Around that time, Blackboard hired a new VP of Quality Engineering. Ashley told us that, when he came on board,

That's when we decided to pause and review our QA. While we had people who believed in a quality culture, it still fell to our testers to be responsible for it. We asked ourselves, "How can we speed up delivery, be more productive, make our lives easier, and move our philosophy of quality from playing a bit part to being the foundation of our culture?"

They gathered everyone into a conference room and visually mapped out how code flowed through the development pipeline, highlighting each of the steps in the process from an engineer's code commit to production deployment. Once they were clear on the development pipeline, they began to overlay their testing processes. With everything on one canvas, they could now see what types of testing they were using and whether they matched the information that the engineer needed at each stage in the pipeline. This drove discussions on which testing methods the team should use at different stages, in order to deliver the feedback the engineers needed as fast as possible.

For instance, right after merging the feature branch into develop, they would need to ensure they hadn't introduced any unintended issues into the codebase. For this, continuous integration tests were the best tool for the job.[39]

In addition to working out when to perform different types of testing, they re-examined every test they ran to measure its business value. "Finally, we got to the point of asking, 'If there were only one test we could run, which would it be?'" she said. By asking that question at each testing iteration, the team prioritized tests by how much value each delivered to the engineer at that time. This enabled them to identify a set of smaller automation tests that they could run in under ten minutes and earlier in their development pipeline to give the engineers faster feedback, so as to gauge if something critical had broken or not.

The iteration loop went from taking a full business day to a coffee break. With the ability to find and address problems faster, the team saw a significant reduction in critical issues that made it into production. Having seen the success of this approach with one of their product lines, they are now replicating this throughout the business.

Although Ashley and her team used this method of optimization for their regression suite, it has a wider application to the whole of the software development lifecycle.

THE REAL DEFINITION OF "CONTINUOUS TESTING"

When people talk about continuous testing, they often only refer to the aspect of running automated tests during the development phase. But in our opinion, that's a limiting view. Automated testing is only one aspect of the software development cycle.

A more appropriate definition of continuous testing would be the ability to continuously test an application at every stage of its lifecycle, from the initial concept through to production and every point in between.

When talking to people about the benefits of testing at different stages in the development process, I often show them an insightful graph created by Capers Jones.[40] It captures when bugs are potentially introduced into the development process versus when they are identified. It then aims to approximate the cost of fixing them based on when they were found.[41]

Jones' research indicates that upwards of 85% of bugs are introduced in the design and build phases of development, sometimes even before a line of code has been written. A bug found post-release could cost $16,000 or more to address. Yet that same bug could have been remedied in these early stages for as little as $25.[42]

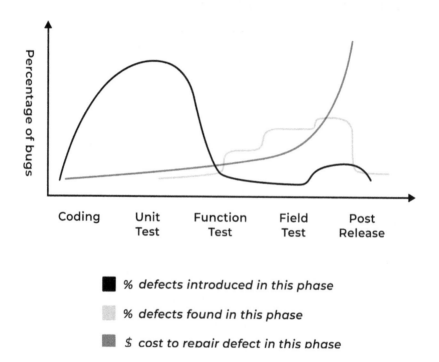

Percentage of bugs

Coding   Unit Test   Function Test   Field Test   Post Release

■ % defects introduced in this phase

▨ % defects found in this phase

■ $ cost to repair defect in this phase

The earlier you can identify and address a problem, the more time and effort it will save you in the long run. That's why it's so important to have the mindset that "continuous testing" applies throughout the development cycle.

Once we are clear that quality teams can help by continuously testing at any point in time,[43] we are able to start working out how to get the most out of different testing approaches.

FEEDBACK LOOPS

In his foundational book on DevOps, *The Phoenix Project*, Gene Kim wrote:

Everyone needs fast feedback loops to prevent problematic code from going into production and to enable code to quickly be deployed into production, so that any production problems are quickly detected and corrected...The competitive advantage this capability creates is enormous, enabling faster feature time to market, increased customer satisfaction, market share, employee productivity, and happiness, as well as allowing organizations to win in the marketplace.

At a high level, the idea of feedback loops reflects the reality of today's competitive business environment. The old method of planning an enormous project, budgeting resources, taking months to create a physical or digital product, and then finally getting it to market just doesn't work for the vast majority of companies today. Markets are continually disrupted to the point that whole industries are transformed in a matter of months or even weeks.

In Chapter 4, we quoted Dan Ashby's comment that "testing is a continuous attempt to uncover information." Feedback loops help us focus on getting information on product quality to the team as fast as possible. A single feedback loop can begin with a trigger event—such as an engineer merging their code to a feature branch, which sets off a testing suite—and end with a form of results (information) that the engineer can use to make a decision. The shorter the feedback loop, the faster a team can respond with changes.

However, when it comes to feedback loops, faster doesn't always mean better. Different types of testing provide different types of information. Just like Ashley at Blackboard, starting by determining what type of feedback you need gives you a better indicator as to what testing type is most suitable.

Elisabeth Hendrickson, the VP of Data R&D at Pivotal Labs, has a great model that focuses on the idea that different types of testing answer different questions:[44]

FEEDBACK NEEDED	TESTING TYPE TO USE
Did I write the code I intended to?	Unit test
Did I write the code I intended to without violating any existing expectations in the code?	Continuous integration tests
Did I introduce any unintended consequences? Are there issues we are not currently aware of?	Exploratory testing
Do the changes in the new build affect the functionality in the current (live) build?	Regression testing
Did I get the feature I asked for?	Acceptance testing
Are we producing something our users love?	User feedback
Is our team headed in the right direction? Do we have confidence that this system will deliver the business value that we asked for?	Stakeholder feedback

As she points out, the feedback loop is different for each of these tests. They have different costs and response times, and return different types of information. A unit test, for example, could quickly return a pass/fail answer, but it couldn't tell much beyond that. Some forms of exploratory testing could take multiple days, but would provide a wealth of insight. Although it would take longer to provide feedback, this doesn't discount its value. Different approaches solve different problems.

Once you have the right feedback loops in place giving you relevant information about the quality of your product, the next step is to work out how to get the information as quickly as possible.

THE FOUR WAYS TO IMPROVE YOUR FEEDBACK LOOPS

There are many different ways to optimize the feedback loops that exist in your testing. From our experience working with some of the best engineering teams in the world, we have seen that they can be grouped into four main areas:

1. Prioritize value over speed.
2. Run tests simultaneously to increase scale.
3. Learn through continuous improvement.
4. Create infrastructure that leverages the team.

Each of these at first may only seem to provide a marginal gain. However, over time, the compounding nature of continuous improvement will start to have a positive effect on the overall efficiency of your testing.

Prioritize Value over Speed

Even though this section is about improving your feedback loops, that doesn't just mean speeding them up. Focusing on the value you get from the feedback can be more important than the speed. It doesn't matter how quickly you can deliver testing results if you're not providing the engineers with the information they need.

In order to improve testing at Blackboard, Ashley and her team didn't reduce the time it took for the regression tests to execute. Instead, they focused on breaking up the testing into smaller sections so that they were running the most valuable tests at the right time.

Run Tests Simultaneously to Increase Scale

If you have ten tests that you run one after the other, the fastest way to improve the speed of the tests is to be able to run them all at the same time. This would mean your total testing time would only be as long as your longest test, as opposed to the length of all the tests added together.

In order to run tests in parallel, it's important to ensure that the tests are as modular and decoupled as possible. This will allow you to scale running your automated tests faster on virtualized cloud environments like Sauce Labs. In cases where you want to accomplish the same scale in real-world environments for tests that you can't automate (or haven't yet automated), using crowdsourced testing providers is a great solution.

Learn through Continuous Improvement

How can teams learn from the past in order to move even faster in the future?

Taking the time to look back on a process to identify the root cause of an issue is called a retrospective. While interviewing Abby Bangser, a senior testing engineer at the online printing company MOO, she told us, "I don't just care about the bug. I want to know where and how that bug was found, what led to its introduction in the first place, and how we can make sure it doesn't happen again."

Abby doesn't just want to find existing bugs; she wants to prevent the same mistakes from happening twice. This reduces the potential for similar bugs to be introduced in the future.

It could be that a release went out without sufficient testing of a key area of your app. Addressing that blind spot would help avoid the same types of bugs occurring in future builds, while eliminating the need for additional iterations altogether.

Create Infrastructure That Leverages the Team

Finally, the best quality teams focus on infrastructure development. They actively look for tools that will allow them to spend more time on high-value activities and less on low-impact tasks.

No matter where your testing is, there are opportunities to improve in all four of these areas. From testing to ensure you're delivering customer value, to making certain a line of an engineer's code does what it was intended to, you can always optimize. And the best way to see the places where there is scope for improvement is to map out your development pipeline and identify what feedback is needed where.

However, feedback loops are a wasted opportunity without the correct infrastructure in place to take advantage of them. In the next chapter, we outline the most effective types of infrastructure you can implement to improve the efficiency of your team.

CHAPTER 6 SUMMARY (TL;DR)

▪ In order to provide true continuous testing, you need to test a product at every stage of its lifecycle, from the initial concept through to testing in production and every point in between.

▪ Have a clear understanding of your development pipeline to know what feedback you need to provide to the engineering team at each stage.

▪ Knowing what information you want from a test determines the type of testing you choose to do.

▪ Each testing type has its own feedback loop that has unique information, costs, and response times.

▪ Having worked with some of the best engineering teams in the world, we've observed that optimizing feedback revolves around four key areas:

1. Prioritize value over speed.
2. Run tests simultaneously to increase scale.
3. Learn through continuous improvement.
4. Create infrastructure that leverages the team.

7| INVESTING IN TESTING INFRASTRUCTURE

"Just like with everything else, tools won't give you good results unless you know how, when, and why to apply them. If you go out and you buy the most expensive frying pan on the market it's still not going to make you a good chef."
Christin Wiedemann

When IoT firm EVRYTHNG hired Charles Adeeko as Director of Quality and Test, fixing critical issues and releasing product updates was taking too long. The team wasn't delivering features to their customers at the right quality level. There was a belief within the company that the implementation of UI automation would speed up the delivery pipeline and fix the outstanding quality issues with the product.[45]

When he got into the trenches, Charles realized that there were issues with both the Ownership Narrative and the "How to Test" Narrative. He could see that he would need to work on how the team thought about the Agile process as well as development and test practices. UI automation alone wasn't going to be the main factor to speed up the delivery process and improve the quality of the product. It would help a little, but the delays weren't coming from tests taking too long. One of the core problems he identified was how long it took to address the issues once they found them.

"What good was testing if nothing could be fixed?" he said.

In order to resolve this, Charles and his team worked on developing a continuous delivery infrastructure that allowed them to quickly get code into production.

In *The Effective Engineer*, author and software engineer Edmond Lau describes his first exposure to working in a continuous integration and continuous delivery environment, which came when he joined the question and answer website Quora:

...when I first joined Quora...I had...concerns. New engineers add themselves to the team page as one of their first tasks, and the notion that the code I wrote on my first day would so easily go into production was exhilarating—and frightening.

He went on to write that a "number of high-leverage investments in our infrastructure made this rapid release cycle possible," including tools that versioned and packaged their code and a system that ran thousands of unit and integration tests in parallel (then immediately tested on web servers, then automatically deployed into production). On top of this, the team built a number of monitoring tools, as well as a robust rollback feature that would let them quickly recall any releases.

But only focusing on deployment speed is risky. What good is it having a team that's set up to release bad code to production even faster? Alongside being able to deploy quickly, teams must have an infrastructure allowing them to monitor what's happening post-deploy and to quickly revert or deploy a new fix if necessary.

If Amazon went down or had a major bug only once in three years but it took an entire day to recover, they would be facing their customers' wrath for months. If Amazon went down three times a day and it took only a second or two to recover, their customers would barely notice.

Utilizing frameworks like continuous delivery provides a foundation for you to implement monitoring and alerting systems, as well as forms of testing in production that can help your team identify issues that may have been missed in earlier forms of testing.

MONITORING FOR IMPACT ON YOUR USERS

Monitoring allows you to observe what is happening in an environment and set alerts or triggers if there is a variance from the expected behavior. For example, a huge drop in traffic after a release may signal that something critical is broken.

When setting up monitoring and alerting systems, it is important to ensure that your team is focused on monitoring the biggest impact on your customers. If not, you may find yourself in a similar position to the quality team at online ticket sales platform Ticketmaster.

The team had set up monitoring on all of their systems, but they were still facing multiple customer-impacting issues either detected too late or, worse still, that came to their attention because of customer support calls.

In their search for best practice, they came across a paper written by Rob Ewaschuk titled "My Philosophy on Alerting," which draws on his seven years of being an on-call engineer at Google.[46] In the paper, he advocates moving from cause-based monitoring to symptom-based monitoring, i.e., "monitoring for impact on your users."

He pointed out that users really care about four things:

1. **Basic availability and correctness**: no "page not found" errors, no missing images or anything that shows unavailability
2. **Latency**: everything loading quickly
3. **Completeness, freshness, and durability:** the data they store with

you being safe and accessible when they want to retrieve it

4. **Features**: the features they want are working correctly

As he put it:

Do your users care if your MySQL servers are down? No; they care if their queries are failing. (Your users don't even know your MySQL servers exist!) Do your users care if a support (i.e., non-serving-path) binary is in a restart loop? No, they care if their features are failing. Do they care if your data push is failing? No, they care about whether their results are fresh.[47]

Based on Rob's paper, Ticketmaster changed their monitoring and alerting process to a more user impact-driven method.[48] They mapped out the most important user flows, such as adding a ticket to the cart, placing an order, and choosing a payment method.

For each flow, they identified observable indicators of pain points for the user, such as error signs, latency, and page timeouts. To ensure alerts reflected the user perspective, they set up the alerts for the front-end web service and the API layer connected to the mobile app.

It is interesting to note that, initially, the Ticketmaster team simply used email for the alert notifications (they could have also chosen messaging platforms like Slack, HipChat, or Microsoft Teams). After tweaking the emails, they saw success as different engineering teams jumped on the alerts. Then they discovered a secondary benefit: the alerts increased communication among all the teams. Because they all received the same emails, they were all constantly and simultaneously aware of the various problems across the application.

Eventually, they moved away from email to a dedicated incident management platform to manage 24/7 alerts, on-call schedules, and escalation policies. When an alert went off, everyone was clear on the impact on the customer and there was little to no pushback from their engineers to be on call to fix the problem. In their words, it was a breeze.

Overall, our shift in focus to symptom-based alerting has paid dividends and has allowed us to detect issues and react faster, making the site more stable and providing a better experience for our fans.[49]

Setting up monitoring and alerts to focus on the impact on customers will keep your teams thinking about what brings value to your customers. It will provide a lagging indicator that informs you of your whole quality process.

If you are constantly being alerted about issues in production, it would be wise to review how you could adjust your process earlier in the development lifecycle.

TESTING IN PRODUCTION

The idea of testing in production used to be associated with amateur programming, shipping things with little to no prior testing and delivering a terrible user experience. However, over the past couple of years, there has been an increasing interest in how testing in production can help improve the quality of a product, while making the systems we build more robust.

Although there are different schools of thought around this, the underlying theme is that most environments that people test in (local, staging, etc.) are not close enough to the production environment. The difference in configurations, data sets, and assets in production environments can alter the experience your end user receives.

Therefore, the closer you can test to the environment a user will be in, the better understanding you have of your product's quality. This is the approach that media companies like *The Guardian* have taken.

A national UK newspaper in print since 1821, *The Guardian* launched its online edition in 1999 and since then has added *Guardian US* and *Guardian Australia*. Across all of their platforms, they now have over 150 million unique visitors a month.

Sally Goble, the former Head of Quality at the iconic paper, talked to us about how she utilized testing in production. For many years, her teams had focused on writing automated tests that ran before shipping to production. But those tests were, in her words, "unreliable and slow with lots of false positives. We were constantly refactoring the automated tests because they were just so flaky."[50]

Because of this, their developers were disengaged in the work the quality teams were doing, not trusting the test results while simultaneously resenting the fact that they slowed down the release process. They had no confidence in the tests themselves and, frankly, didn't want to waste time executing them.

In response, Sally began to think about QA from a lean perspective. Her team's main objective was to improve the quality of the product without slowing down the release process.

If the team had a solid infrastructure in place that allowed them to continually deploy, monitor if there were any changes in core metrics, and roll back if there was a problem, they could take the risk of finding the problems later in the process even if that meant post-release.

The team began to experiment with keeping a smaller set of core tests that would run in the development phase, but started to move toward more monitoring and automated testing in production. As everyone in the development and quality teams became more comfortable with the idea, they started to notice improvements. Quality teams had more time to focus on the most critical parts of the product. Engineers saw more value in the testing that was happening, as they were getting the right type of feedback they needed at each stage of the development process.

One member of her former team, Jacob Winch, put it like this:

We believe developers should derive confidence from knowing their code has run successfully in the real world, rather than from observing green test cases in a sanitized environment. We minimized testing run pre-deployment and extended our deployment pipeline to include feedback on tests run against the production site.

A complete shift in their quality narrative.

However, not everyone has the risk tolerance to work in the way Sally and her team did. Simpler forms of testing in production may include introducing canary releases into your process.

The term "canary release" comes from the saying "a canary in a coal mine." This is a reference to the old mining practice of bringing a caged bird into a coal shaft. If the air turned bad and oxygen was low, the bird would stop singing and quickly die—an early warning to the miners that something was dangerously wrong.

A canary release involves rolling out a feature on a limited basis, whether to the internal team dogfooding the product or to a small subset of users. If they have positive feedback, they roll the release out to the rest of their users. If they get negative feedback, the company can roll back the change to the previous build and test the new release further, thereby limiting the number of affected people to a fraction of their customers.

TESTING IN PRODUCTION TOO SOON

In a *Medium* article titled "Testing in Production, the safe way,"[51] Cindy Sridharan, the author of *Distributed Systems Observability*, highlights that testing in production requires a more advanced infrastructure setup to execute properly.

I'd argue that being able to successfully and safely test in production requires a significant amount of automation, a firm understanding of the best practices as well as designing the systems from the ground up to lend themselves well toward this form of testing.

It's important to note, however, that testing in production doesn't make sense for every product and isn't a replacement for doing other forms of testing. It's just yet another tool to gather information along the continuous testing spectrum. When used as a single source of testing, things can go very, very wrong. Something OkCupid found out the hard way.

When OkCupid was still a small company, the then CEO, Mike Maxim, told the team, "We can't sacrifice forward momentum for technical debt."[52] Testing frameworks were thought of as "somewhat academic, more lofty than practical."

Their primary way of testing was just to send things to a small subset of production users and see what happened. Were there crashes? Were users complaining? Like *The Guardian*, they figured that if something went wrong, they would do a rollback or respond with a quick patch.

When junior engineer Dale Markowitz joined, she was asked to build a small feature and push it to production. After she did and reviewed the metrics on a small subset of users, she pushed it out to the rest of the site. When she returned from her break, something was wrong. The site had ground to a halt and all of OkCupid's servers were offline. Per usual, multiple engineers had pushed code to production at the same time. But, without the proper infrastructure to quickly sift through the multiple commits, the team was struggling to determine where the issue was. Eventually, they discovered that an untested part of Dale's code was the culprit, but the site was down for over an hour, an eternity for an online B2C service like theirs.

When we spoke with Meaghan Lewis, an Engineering Manager at GitHub, she reiterated the importance of investing in improving quality before production:

It's better to have testing processes in place beforehand and have them happen regularly during development. By the time you actually do the release, you will already have the confidence to ship.[53]

When speaking with our own quality team, I often say, "The role of quality isn't over until it's fixed for the user." I seek to highlight that quality isn't just about testing, and deploying faster doesn't mean you should deploy bad code faster.

Once code is in production, it's important to remember that the infrastructure should be there to support your customer having the best experience of your product. This holds true whether you find yourself in the early stages of setting up an infrastructure like Charles (from EVRYTHNG) where you are focusing on continuous delivery to get new features and bug fixes deployed faster, or at a more advanced point like Sally from *The Guardian*—where you are focusing on monitoring and testing.

CHAPTER 7 SUMMARY (TL;DR)

■ Improving quality in your company goes far beyond testing. It includes having an infrastructure that allows issues to be fixed quickly.

■ Implementing continuous delivery allows you to quickly release and to roll back if problems are identified in production.

■ Monitoring and alerting systems should be "symptom-based" instead of "cause-based." This ensures that your team are focused on the impact on users.

■ Testing in production allows you to test in the most similar environment to what your users will be using, giving you the best understanding of your product's quality.

■ Testing in production requires having a firm understanding of best practice, and shouldn't be the only form of testing done.

SECTION III

LEADING YOUR TEAM TO ACCELERATE GROWTH

8 | ALIGN YOUR TEAM TO YOUR COMPANY GROWTH METRIC

"You don't grow a business on increased activity. You don't generate revenue by selling story points. You grow a business on outcomes, such as new features delivered that are valued by your customers." [54]

Melanie Ziegler, founder of VPE Forum

A few years ago, I had lunch in New York with a young QA engineer. He worked for a company that created absolutely stunning virtual reality tours for university campuses. During the conversation, I asked him which core metric his team was working toward.[55]

"Zero bugs," he said with no hesitation.

Fortunately, he didn't see the look of disbelief on my face. I was worried for him and his team. Zero bugs is not only virtually impossible for a high-growth startup to achieve, but it's entirely the wrong focus.

"And how did you work that out?" I asked in a neutral tone.

His response echoed what we'd heard before: the CTO had come under fire because of the number of problems customers had reported in the latest release, so he had set a goal of zero bugs as the metric for the quality team.

Choosing a metric like that is bad for two reasons. First, the focus wasn't on value. Was "zero bugs" going to bring the biggest value to the business? Would it help them grow? Was fixing every bug important for the customer?

Second, as he explained the dynamics of the metric in detail, I learned that it had only been given to the test teams. The Ownership Narrative was all wrong. It disregarded the role that all the other teams played in the reduction of bugs.

As we sat there discussing ideas about aligning the operational work that he did with potential business goals, he asked a question that Owais and I get asked often when we speak at conferences: "How can you connect QA to business metrics when QA is just a support function?"

When this question comes up, we normally answer with another question: "Inside your company right now, what's the core metric you use to measure how the company is going to grow?"

The standard responses are usually sales, profit, revenue, number of active users, or some other outcome-led metric. Then we ask a follow-up question: "Now, what kind of success metrics do you have for your testing team?"

Common answers include the time it takes to run test cases or the number of bugs found. In other words, activity-based metrics. The problem with them is that it's difficult to measure how those QA activities support the outcome-led metrics the business is driven by. This usually results in a lightbulb moment where members of the audience see how their testing team are measuring things that aren't impactful.

In *The Lean Startup*, author Eric Ries calls these "vanity metrics." Numbers that make you feel like you're getting results but are hard to action on and don't correlate to the success of the business. On top of metrics like "bugs found," other types of vanity metrics include registered users, downloads, or raw number of pageviews. They sound impressive and may even look good (especially when everything's going right). But do your customers really care how many bugs you found? Do they care that you cut your automation suite runtime in half? Those are indirect measures of things that ultimately matter: active users within a time period, engagement, cost per new customer, or profit.

Compare the typical answers to the questions regarding a company's business metrics and quality metrics. You'll immediately see the disconnect between how they measure business success and QA success. The business metric focuses on a quantifiable result. The quality team's metric focuses on action rather than outcome and typically has little measurable effect on the business outcomes.

You can cut your testing time in half and see zero effect on sales or revenue. You can decrease the number of bugs found to nearly nothing and not see a spike in your number of active users. Ultimately, the metrics your testing team focus on should improve overall company growth.

The final question we ask when speaking at conferences is:

"Which metrics can your team affect that will have the biggest impact on your company?"

That question reframes the whole dynamic by bridging the gap between growing the overall business and the focus of the quality teams. Instead of seeing QA as a support function, it turns QA into a growth driver.

Put another way: how can your quality teams help your company grow?

THE ONE METRIC THAT DRIVES ALL OTHERS

When Ilya Sakharov joined HelloFresh, the world's largest meal kit company, as Director of Quality Assurance, he quickly discovered that his quality team were completely disconnected from the rest of the business.[56]

From conversations with different departments, it was clear that a communication gap had arisen, whereby the quality team were developing test strategies with no connection to what was important to the company and it was affecting inter-departmental relationships.

To make changes, Ilya knew it was critical to get alignment between all teams. For HelloFresh, this was done through OKRs (Objectives and Key Results),[57] a goal-setting framework pioneered by Intel's Andy Grove and adopted by companies like Google. The most important metric for HelloFresh was the number of recipe box subscribers.

Ilya's first step was to make sure that his teams were being exposed to the data on the number of subscribers and that they understood why it was important. Next, he encouraged his teams to begin speaking in terms of the effect that situations would have on the number of subscribers. This meant that when they performed risk-based analysis on where to test, they focused on areas that would have a greater impact on the subscriber metric. Even though the idea was new to them, they got it and started to think about new ways to impact the metric.

For example, a critical part of HelloFresh's development infrastructure involves using A/B testing to optimize conversion rates across the platform. Due to the iterative nature of the A/B tests, the code wasn't as clean as the rest of their codebase. This wasn't a problem when a test failed and the code was removed, but it became a problem when a test passed and the winning test would be merged into production. By having a focus on what was affecting the subscription metric, the quality team paid more attention to the significance of A/B tests than they would have previously.

Ilya also noticed a change in his teams' attitude toward work. Their motivation picked up, as they were clearer on how they contributed to the company's success. Product management and engineering teams also noticed the difference and the cross-functional relationships between all departments strengthened.

Alignment around a single common goal can reduce conflicts between teams. The conversation between the quality team at HelloFresh and the rest of the business became smoother because there was more clarity on how the quality team contributed to the bigger picture. Perhaps more importantly, though, the company saw a reduction in the amount of critical issues reaching production.

Ilya's focus on "subscribers to recipe boxes" echoes the story that we recounted in Chapter 1 regarding uSwitch CTO Mike Jones, who aligned his quality and engineering teams around the "number of switches" metric with similar outcomes. They both kept their teams focused on what was important.

But how do you know which number to focus on? What we've observed is that the best companies have a single company-wide metric that drives every decision, every department, and every individual's efforts.

We call it the "growth metric."

HOW TO IDENTIFY THE RIGHT GROWTH METRIC FOR YOUR TEAM

Some people, like Ilya, are lucky to have a growth metric clearly communicated by the leadership team using frameworks like OKRs, but for others, it isn't always as clear which metrics to focus on.

Whether you are in an enterprise where it makes more sense to deviate toward a submetric or department-based metric, or the existing metrics in your company are too vague, the key thing is to determine which growth metric will bring the most value to your company.

Product analytics company Amplitude reviewed metrics from over 11,000 companies and determined that there were three main types of growth metrics:[59] attention-based, transaction-based, and productivity-based.

Attention-Based Growth Metrics

If your product is primarily used for entertainment or information, like many B2C companies in the media and gaming industry, then you might want to consider using an attention-based growth metric. Attention-based growth metrics focus on the amount of time the user spends on the platform.

Many consumer internet companies often use the growth metric of daily active users (DAUs). Focusing on DAUs not only lets their internal teams concentrate on getting users to engage with the product on a daily basis (i.e., ensuring the platform is valuable enough for them to come back every day), but also supports the business by increasing their revenue possibilities.

With Netflix, you might imagine their core growth metric to be the number of films watched or subscription revenue. But the former Chief Product Officer, Neil Hunt, revealed that the streaming service gauges success by a variation of viewing hours called "valued hours."

This isn't simply a tally of how many hours people spend watching a show. Instead, it measures each show's success based on the number of hours of a show that are viewed relative to the user's total viewing hours.

If a certain show makes up a disproportionate part of someone's viewing habits, then that show must be really important to them. At the fringes, this becomes quite revealing: there are some subscribers who watch almost nothing else but a certain show. As such, they're effectively paying Netflix to access only one show. The more valued hours a show aggregates, the more successful Netflix deems it to be.

Transaction-Based Growth Metrics

Other companies' users find value primarily in using the product to purchase goods or services, as in the case of e-commerce, subscription, or marketplace platforms. Effective growth metrics for these types of businesses focus on optimizing the experience and reducing the friction of purchase.

Marketplaces like Airbnb look at measuring the point where the buyer (a guest) and the seller (a host) transact by making a booking. By measuring the number of nights booked as their core metric, Airbnb can capture the point where both users get the most value out of using the product. For Uber and Lyft, a similar metric would be rides completed, again serving both the buyer (passengers) and the sellers (drivers) equally.

Productivity-Based Growth Metrics

For products used in the B2B space, the software itself usually aids a customer to complete a digital task or workflow. By using the software, the customer is aiming to improve their own productivity. This is where metrics based on user activity often serve well. This means your team should be focused on how quickly the user can reach success at a given task.

For Slack, the fastest-growing enterprise tech company ever,[61] their growth metric is the number of teams that have sent over 2,000 messages. In the words of their CEO and cofounder, Stewart Butterfield:

Based on experience of which companies stuck with us and which didn't, we decided that any team that has exchanged 2,000 messages in its history has tried Slack—really tried it... It hit us that, regardless of any other factor, after 2,000 messages, 93% of those customers are still using Slack today.[62]

Think of how clear a goal that is: "How can we get more teams to send over 2,000 messages? What quality issues are blocking that?"

To determine your growth metric, first pick one of the three metric types. Even though there may be more than one that suits your company, try to find the one that resonates the most.

Next, write down how your customer gets value from using your product. Once you have a few ideas, try to whittle it down to a single growth metric that you think will have the biggest impact on your company. If you get stuck, try focusing on a different growth metric type to see if it sparks any new ideas.[63]

But what about your other metrics? In reliability engineering teams, they often use a metric called mean time to recovery (MTTR). It looks at how long it takes, on average, to fix something once there's a problem or even an outage. What's great about this metric is that it doesn't count how many outages happened. It focuses on how long the problem persisted for. Why? Because that's what your users really care about.

That's just one example of the other indicators you need to watch. The goal of the growth metric isn't to replace all your other metrics. You should absolutely use all the information you can to manage your teams and move the business forward. A good growth metric, however, will let you and your teams focus on moving what really matters—a metric that, when you improve it, will move all the other critical metrics in the right direction.

HOW YOUR GROWTH METRIC IMPACTS TESTING

Once you have your growth metric, you can then determine how it changes your approach to quality. The first thing it should do is inform how you prioritize quality issues. The issues that impact the metric are the ones you focus on first.

For the European budget airline Wizz Air, the focus is on the number of flights booked. When their quality teams look through bugs and other identified issues, they rank them according to how they affect conversion to a flight booking. Their whole outlook is now focused on becoming a conversion-led company, which trickles down to their quality team.

Referring back to HelloFresh, when questioning whether an issue should be prioritized the team might ask themselves questions that revolve around their growth metric of number of recipe box subscribers.

For example:

- How many of our subscribers does this issue currently affect?
- How many potential subscribers could it be affecting?
- What would be the impact on subscribers if it was fixed?

By asking these questions the team are able to connect the work they do to a core business metric; they can accurately communicate, to themselves, their colleagues, and managers, just how valuable their efforts are.

Then the teams crunch the numbers to estimate how much a given task would positively affect those numbers. Once they implement the change, they monitor to see if it actually moved the metric as expected or not.

This allows the quality teams to connect the work they do to a core business metric; they can accurately communicate, to themselves, their colleagues, and managers, just how valuable their efforts are.

The second thing your growth metric can do is increase cross-functional teamwork, as Sean Ellis, the godfather of growth hacking, witnessed. When Sean was the VP of Marketing at LogMeIn, they discovered that 95% of new LogMeIn signups never once used the service for a remote-control session.

It wasn't until engineering, product, and marketing pulled together to focus on the signup-to-usage rate, which required a bunch of experimentation and took months, that we saw the business start to hockey-stick. We were able to get 1,000% improvement in the signup-to-usage rate.[64]

That's the kind of measure you're looking for.

A good growth metric sits at a high enough level that no single team moves it all by themselves. Having this shared goal allows the quality teams to interact with other teams, like working with data scientists to get more accurate information about user behavior or working alongside the customer support teams to access helpdesk chat.

To be an effective leader, you have to be clear about what your team's doing and where you're going. Growth metrics allow you to focus your team on high-impact tasks that grow the company. When you focus on measuring outputs and activities—as so many organizations measure testing progress—teams can get lost in busywork. By measuring outcome-led metrics, you stand a greater chance of contributing to business growth in a positive way.

Let your growth metric become your guiding star as you lead quality in your company.

CHAPTER 8 SUMMARY (TL;DR)

▪ A growth metric is the one metric that has the greatest impact on growth in your company and is where your customer gets the most value from your product.

▪ Growth metrics can be broken down into three broad categories:

  ▪ **Attention-based**, most commonly used by B2C companies

  ▪ **Transaction-based**, most commonly used by e-commerce and marketplace companies

  ▪ **Productivity-based**, most commonly used by B2B companies

▪ To identify your growth metric, find out what the core value you provide to your customer is and use that as your measurement.

▪ Once you have identified what your company's growth metric should be, begin to focus all quality activities on moving the metric. This allows you to align your teams around what helps the company grow.

WANT HELP WORKING OUT YOUR GROWTH METRIC?

You can download our worksheet at:

lqbook.co/resources

9 | DRIVING GROWTH WITH LOCAL PERSONAS

"One of the things I've always found is that you've got to start with the customer experience, and work backwards for the technology."

Steve Jobs

Airbnb engineers travel. A lot.

Much of this is because the company practice "empathy engineering," whereby engineers spend time with customers and those directly supporting them so they can understand the customer mindset when developing out products and features.

On one particular trip, engineer Dmitry Alexeenko flew to Portland, Oregon to spend time with the customer support teams and agents. By doing so, he got a better understanding of the issues that customers were dealing with.[65]

Dmitry's travel afterwards saw multiple trips along the Asian-Pacific Rim, including Tokyo, Seoul, and Singapore. The investment in empathy engineering paid off: Dmitry immediately began noticing the significant differences as he went from West to East, and especially in how people used the Airbnb apps.

He saw people using devices he'd never heard of, from brands such as Oppo, ZTE, and Vivo. In Seoul, he noted that the online payment process was more complex than he was accustomed to. Researching further, he discovered that the South Korean government had passed a law in 1999 that meant that online payments could only be completed through an old version of Internet Explorer with ActiveX enabled (a predecessor to Microsoft's Edge browser).[66]

In Japan, the messaging apps were designed differently, using manga-style icons and stickers in place of the cartoon-like ones Dmitry was accustomed to in the West. Throughout the region, instead of sleek, minimal-design web pages with functionality discreetly hidden away, they were busy and displayed an array of options up front.

These trips gave Dmitry a new perspective on Airbnb customers: his team did not build and test things for a single, homogenous market, but rather a fast-expanding global market comprising multiple user personas.

If your team is now focused on moving toward a growth metric, you'll begin to notice that thinking from a customer's viewpoint becomes more and more important. That's because your growth metric represents the moment the customer receives value from your product.

When your company is growing globally, it becomes more difficult to understand how users are experiencing your product. Your team needs to understand a more nuanced user persona called a "local persona." Once your team has identified each user's device, OS, and location, they can begin to work out how to test in an environment as close to the persona as possible.

LOCAL PERSONAS – KNOWING WHO YOUR CUSTOMERS ARE

Marketing and product departments constantly ask, "Who is our customer?" to help them hone their message and ensure they are building the product for the right person. They create broad personas like Owner Ollie, Marketing Mary, and Enterprise Erin[67] to outline the identity of their average customer.

Once these personas have been created, it's tempting to use them across the entire company. For engineering and quality teams, however, your real users' experiences are more diverse and complex than these simplified personas.

Every device, every operating system, and every location creates a new experience for how your customer uses your app...and when a new user opens it for the first time, they expect it to work perfectly for them.

When GoDaddy's Chief Platform and Globalization Officer, James Carroll, faced the task of successfully launching into 125 countries in three years, he quickly realized that the only way to reach the kind of growth he needed was to tailor the business to suit the local market: "You have to really show up as local. In every single touchpoint of your experience with a company. You have to offer locally relevant products."[68]

The more diverse (geographically and by device type) your user base is, the more important it is to be able to localize your testing to ensure your product works for each of your local personas.

But how does this knowledge accelerate growth?

FINDING YOUR LOCAL PERSONAS TO SUPPORT GROWTH

In order to grow a company, you not only need to be able to acquire new customers; you also have to retain and expand the revenue from the ones that you already have. When using local personas to help move a growth metric, most companies start by looking at their existing customers first. Whether your product teams are focused on new features to increase engagement or working out how to increase the value the customers get from the product so they spend more, the aim is to make sure you're not filling a leaking bucket.

The second area to look at is new customer acquisition, focusing on the onboarding experience and getting users to your "aha" moment—where they really understand the value of the product—as fast as possible.

For both areas, the concept of local personas can be useful for thinking about how you approach testing to move a growth metric.

Retention and Expansion

If your company has a focus on retaining or expanding existing customers, you'll first need to understand what your current local persona looks like. Internal analytics tools such as Google Analytics or AppDynamics will give you information on the device, operating system, and location that your existing customers are using. From there, you can pick the ones that make up the largest market share to base your local personas on and guide your testing.

It's also important to note that your internal data might not always be giving you the full picture. There are times when existing customers are trying to use your product on devices that you are not properly supporting but the experience is so bad that they have defaulted to using your product on the devices that are working.

New Customer Acquisition

Are your potential new customers the same as your old ones?

A common mistake that people make when using local personas is assuming that the new customers they want to acquire are going to have the exact same local personas as their existing customers. Although this can sometimes be true, many times (particularly when a company enter a brand-new market) the local personas are completely different.

For example, some countries have country-specific devices and proprietary operating systems built on Android. You might run into Indus OS in India, Tizen OS in Vietnam, or LineageOS in Russia. Your applications will act differently in each of these locations.

When online survey company SurveyMonkey began to grow beyond its native market, CTO Selina Tobaccowala's team had to rethink their approach to even the simplest things like text boxes: "English is short. On average, every other language takes one and a half times the length of the same thing said in English."[69] Her design and engineering teams started leaving 50% more space to avoid truncation problems in other languages.

In order to better understand the local personas when entering new markets, we suggest you also use external benchmark services like DeviceAtlas or Opensignal to discover which device and OS combinations are most popular in those countries.

Once you're clear on where to focus your testing, you can then start to choose the best method to test a local experience.

TESTING THE LOCAL EXPERIENCE

Whether your local personas have multiple devices, multiple locations, or a mixture of both, testing local personas can sometimes seem complex and even overwhelming.

If your local personas have a wide range of devices, you have to support a never-ending list of OS release updates as well as new devices throughout the year. If your local personas are in multiple locations, the problem is compounded by language differences and network carriers who can affect your customers' experience.

If your product was being used in Nigeria, testing it inside your office with fiber optic or Wi-Fi, or running your app on an emulator, gives you a limited perspective and ability to identify problems compared to someone in the country downloading your app on a 2G network.

The best way to test a local persona is in the real world, as close to the environment of your current users as possible.

When determining how to test in those environments, there are a few questions that you should ask yourself:

- How can you make the whole process as repeatable and scalable as the rest of your testing infrastructure?
- How can you optimize the feedback loop between needing information about a local persona and having it ready for your team to use?
- Which environments (staging/production) make the most sense for you to be testing in?

These questions will help give you a clearer idea as to which approach you need. Potential ideas include sending your team to the location to test, using your existing users, or working with an external partner.

Send Your Team to the Location

Sending your team to a country with a handful of devices (or having them buy them once they arrive) can be a great way to test in the same environments as your local personas. Just like we saw from Dmitry's time in Tokyo, Seoul, and Singapore, being on-site creates a level of understanding and customer empathy that simply can't be reached any other way.

However, due to the time and expense of travel, this method becomes harder to use if you want to have a more repeatable process to test all of your key locations at the same time. You also don't have the local knowledge of someone who lives there, who will be able to identify more localized issues.

Use Your Existing Users

In Chapter 5, we touched on using beta users to help support testing. To get this right, it's important that you build a community around your beta users.

Google Maps have done a fantastic job of recruiting users and developing a community to help them check and improve the product locally. These volunteers proudly provide their time to enhance the local Google Maps experience.[70] Known as "Local Guides," they do everything from updating street changes to tagging wheelchair-accessible cafés.

Local Guides who have reached Level 5 and above—according to the internal scoring system—also get access to pre-release features, such as AR navigation, to test and report any bugs or issues they find along the way.[71]

Given the right training, support, and coordination, beta users can help test your product and provide local knowledge that would be hard to come by otherwise. However, the drawback comes from the overhead of managing the community, as well as the fact that your users are volunteers who may not have the time or the technical background to ensure they are providing you with crash logs and clear steps to reproduce when you need them.

Work with External Partners

The market need for professional testing in real-world conditions presented a problem for companies. The obvious solution of flying their in-house teams to each location posed too much of an operational burden; this created an opportunity for a number of crowdsourced testing providers to develop an offering that allowed testing locally on a mixture of devices and operating systems.

A crowd offers the depth and breadth of professional testing in any country and any device/OS combination you've identified through your local personas. However, not all crowdsourced testing providers are the same. Some focus specifically on working with professional testers to ensure quality, while others include non-testers to deliver a larger crowd size. The latter can result in poor-quality tests as, in effect, you are hiring non-experts to do an expert's job.

The company's long-term direction and focus must also be taken into consideration. The very nature of testing requires providers to be agile. Technology evolves at a rapid pace, so innovation is important. They should be interested in integrating deeper into your development process, not just finding bugs with local testers.[*]

No matter how you decide to test your local personas, what's essential is ensuring that your team is considering them in your testing strategy. Testing in an environment as close to the customer's as possible will always give you the clearest view on what the quality level of your product is for your customer.

---

[*] To find out more about how we look at being a long-term partner, check out www.globalapptesting.com.

CHAPTER 9 SUMMARY (TL;DR)

- Every device, every operating system, and every location creates a new experience for how your customer uses your app.
- In order to ensure your customers are experiencing the quality that they want, you should aim to test in real-world conditions.
- In order to test in the environments of your local personas, you can choose to:
  - Send your team to the location to test on the ground
  - Use your existing users as beta users to test the product
  - Work with an external partner such as crowdsourced testing vendors

10 | LEADING QUALITY STRATEGY

"Vision and strategy are both important. But there is a priority to them. Vision always comes first. Always. If you have a clear vision, you will eventually attract the right strategy. If you don't have a clear vision, no strategy will save you."[72]
Michael Hyatt

In 2000, Michael Hyatt was promoted to Publisher of Nelson Books, one of fourteen divisions within the historic Thomas Nelson publishing house. Unfortunately, the promotion came about because his boss had resigned. This was hardly a shock, since Nelson Books was by far the worst-performing of Thomas Nelson's fourteen divisions.

In the previous three years, revenue had flatlined. In the most recent year, the division had actually lost money. On top of that, their biggest author had just signed with another publishing house. The outlook was already desperate and now looking increasingly worse.

People in the other thirteen divisions grumbled about Nelson Books dragging down the entire company. Within the Nelson Books team, morale was unsurprisingly low. The team worried about the future.

As you might have guessed from the opening quote, Michael didn't start by coming up with a plan. He started by getting crystal clear with a vision: a vision of the future that excited him. He believed that if he could be excited about the picture he painted of the future, his team could get excited, too.

He gathered his people together and laid out what he envisioned happening within the following three years:

- We have ten "franchise authors" whose new books sell at least 100,000 copies in the first 12 months.
- We have ten "emerging authors" whose new books sell at least 50,000 copies in the first 12 months.
- Authors are soliciting other authors on our behalf because they are so excited to be working with us.
- We place at least four books a year on the New York Times bestseller list.
- Our employees consistently "max out" their bonus plans.

He then began sharing it with people throughout Thomas Nelson. They immediately started asking questions like "How in the world are you going to accomplish this!?"

It felt overly ambitious, even for those in profitable divisions. But he believed that if his team knew where they were going, figuring out how to get there would be the easier task.

The team didn't get there in three years; it took just eighteen months.

I love this story. It's not a tech story of a Silicon Valley unicorn. It's about an underdog team in a dying industry that had very little hope left but by staying focused on where they wanted to go, beat the odds and turned things around.

In this final chapter, we're going to use all of the ideas you've learned in this book to inform your QA strategy. To truly lead quality in your company, you will need to follow in Michael Hyatt's footsteps. Create a crystal-clear vision of where you're going, understand your starting point, and evaluate the multiple paths you can choose that define your strategy.

STEP 1 – SETTING THE VISION

Vision is the ability to describe a future picture so clearly that another person can see and understand it. Before you share a vision of your department to your team and peers, you first need to make sure that you're passionate about that vision and that it excites you. But you can't get excited about the future of your team or company if you're not clear about where you see your own future. That's why we have to begin with a slightly different vision, the vision you have for yourself.

Defining Your Vision

In Simon Sinek's now famous TED talk, "How great leaders inspire action,"[74] he points out that all great leaders start with a clear understanding of why they do what they do.

Think back to a time when you were at a crossroads in your life. Or, worse, when you really had no direction at all. How motivated did you feel to work or make decisions? Probably not very motivated at all. It's hard to feel motivated when you don't have clarity of direction. You lose your "why."

Compare that to a moment in time when you were excited and filled with a sense of purpose and direction. What was the difference between those two? My guess is that you saw where you were going and knew how it would benefit you; you had clarity of vision and knew your "why."

When I sat down with a VP of Engineering for a global e-commerce company, he told me that his vision was to leave a legacy in his company, whereby the next person to take his role would look at what he had created and comment on the incredible infrastructure he had put in place. He was excited by this and that vision pushed him to go the extra mile every day in a way that would ensure his vision came true.

To set your personal vision, take some time to write down your ideal future. If you could go forward one, three, or ten years from now, what would your life look like?

- What type of leader are you?
- What legacy did you leave behind in your current role?
- What career trajectory did you take to get to where you are now?
- What skills did you develop over that time?

By thinking with the end in mind, it not only becomes clearer what choices you have to make today, but also makes you better at communicating your intentions to others and gives you extra motivation to push when things get hard.

Is It Aligned with Your Company?

Now that you know your personal direction, take a look at your current company. Where is it planning to go? Reflecting on your company's direction helps you in two ways. First, it lets you assess if the company is the right vehicle to take you in the direction of your vision. If you can't see the connection, then how motivated are you going to be?

Second, as you think about how to better lead your team, the company vision and direction set the context and boundaries for you to work in.

If your company were planning to grow threefold next year, you would need to think about your team, resources, and infrastructure very differently than if it were planning half of that growth. The more you understand about your company's direction, the better equipped you'll be to make strategic decisions around your department.

Once you are clear about the company vision and feel personally aligned to it, you can start to think about the vision for your department.

Building & Communicating a Department Vision

To work out a department vision, we ask similar questions to the ones we posed for the personal vision. The one adjustment is that we only look forward one or two years.* If you could go forward one or two years from now, what do things look like?

- What are the major milestones you have accomplished?
- How has the quality narrative changed inside your company?
- What is the dynamic like inside your team and between other departments?

The answers to these questions become the vision for your department, which you should share and communicate with your team.

Once you have a clear vision for yourself and your department, one that ties into the company's future, you can move onto the second step of assessing your starting point.

STEP 2 – ASSESSING YOUR STARTING POINT

When traveling to a new destination, a map can only help you if you know both where you are going and where you are right now. When it comes to defining your QA strategy, having an assessment of your current situation is extremely useful.

Below is an outline of some of the core areas that you should assess with your team. Gathering this information takes time, but the more you know before you begin your strategic planning, the better.

Your Current Quality Narrative

What is the current quality narrative inside your company?

In Chapter 2, we discussed the three types of quality narrative: the

---

* This is mainly due to the rate of change in modern companies, where company-level strategies adjust every few years, making it difficult to plan past one to two years at a department level.

Ownership Narrative, "How to Test" Narrative, and Value Narrative. To get a better understanding of what the current narrative inside your company is, speak to different members of staff to find out where people currently think your quality levels are or ask each member of your team to write down the top three comments they hear about quality around the business.

Do they look at it as a necessary evil? The bottleneck for delivery? A valued part of the bigger team? You need to pinpoint frustrations and potential resistance to change.

The Current Product Maturity

In Chapter 5, we talked through how quality changes with product maturity. Inside your company, you may have multiple products at different stages. For each product write down its current stage:

- Validation stage: trying to find product-market fit
- Predictability stage: beginning to automate the product more and solidify the infrastructure
- Scaling stage: starting to think about how the quality team can unlock growth for the product

This information will be used later to ensure that you're doing the right type of testing for each stage.

Your Current Process

What's the existing process in your quality team? What feedback do your engineers need at different stages of their development pipeline? Think back to Chapter 6, where we explained how Ashley from Blackboard mapped out their development pipeline and overlaid the testing process on top. We suggest doing something similar. Gather your team in a room and map out your own process. For a more detailed walkthrough on how to do this, check out Ashley's slides and materials at **lqbook.co/ashley**.

Your Company Growth Metric

In Chapter 8, we covered your company growth metric, a metric that is based on the point where your customers get the greatest level of value from using your product. What is the core growth metric your team should be focused on? What type of growth metric best suits your company and product? Attention-based, transaction-based, or productivity-based? When we move into working out the strategy, we will look at how we can use that metric to affect our testing efforts.

Your Local Personas

In Chapter 9, we discussed the fact that every device, every operating system, and every location creates a new experience for how your customer uses your app. What are your existing local personas? Is there a priority order of personas? Is your company focused on retention and expansion or new customer acquisition? What does the local persona of future customers look like? This will help you later identify how you can test closer to your local personas' environments.

Your Team's Skill and Capacity

In addition, you'll also need to assess your team's current capabilities and bandwidth, individually and collectively. Do you have people with the right skill sets and outlook to help you move your growth metric?

With a full understanding of where you are going and where you are right now, you can now begin to work with your team to define a quality strategy.

STEP 3 – WORKING OUT THE STRATEGY

In a restaurant overlooking London, a silver-haired executive gave me an analogy about strategy I'll never forget. He said:

Strategy: it's like being dropped in the middle of the ocean with your team. There's fog all around you. With limited resources, you must come up with a plan to find your way to The Island, a vague place you've never been. If you're not confused while doing the process, you're probably not doing it right.

No matter how many times you've done it, working out your strategy is hard. It involves thinking, really thinking. There are many questions to answer when it comes to defining your QA strategy and the best way to do it is to get the maximum number of brains on the problems.

Share the assessment information you created in the previous stage with everyone who will be involved in the strategy conversation. Give them time to prepare and do their own research before the discussion. Here are a few questions you might want to discuss:*

Quality Narrative Questions

- How would we like to change our quality narrative?
- Which individuals or departments do we need to influence or begin to know in order to start making that change?

(continued)

---

* A more detailed list of questions can be found at lqbook.co/resources.

Testing Questions

- What testing types make the most sense for our product's current stage?
- How can we optimize the feedback loops of our testing so that our engineers get the most value from them?
- How can we test closer to the environments of our local personas?

Value Questions

- What can we do to help move the company growth metric?

Team Skill and Capacity Questions

- What additional training is needed for your team?
- Do we need to reach outside our company to external partners to increase the team's capabilities or capacity?
- Where can we utilize external partners to fill in short- or long-term gaps?

Once you are confident in your strategy, you may realize that you require more resources than originally planned. When articulating back to the management team, remember to use the Value Narrative from Chapter 2, i.e., presenting the revenue potential, savings, and risk mitigation. To make an even stronger case, make sure you use the methods of influence that we outlined in Chapter 3.

Be Ready to Adapt

After you've clarified your vision and understand where you are and how to get there with the resources you have, you'll be truly ready to lead quality in your company.

As you implement these steps, you'll need to continually recalibrate your plans, as all good leaders do. Like one of our favorite authors, Napoleon Hill says: "When defeat comes, accept it as a signal that your plans are not sound, rebuild those plans, and set sail once more toward your coveted goal."[75]

We understand this more than most. We started off all those years ago building a company in the beauty industry. Now, here we are, writing a book on how to lead quality. It's taken years, but if we can pivot our way to where we are now, so can you.

CHAPTER 10 SUMMARY (TL;DR)

- Vision comes first: if you have a clear vision, you will eventually attract the right strategy. If you don't have a clear vision, no strategy will save you.
- To set vision, you need to start with yourself, then make sure it's aligned to your company and then your team/department.
- Assess your starting point of where you are now and where you want to be to understand what's important for your strategy. Use our online resources if you need help.
- Remember, if you're not confused while thinking through your strategy process, you're probably not doing it right.
- Take into account your resource constraints and what you need to get to where you want.
- It's OK to pivot and adjust your strategy if it's not working.

WANT HELP WORKING OUT YOUR PERSONAL AND DEPARTMENTAL VISION?

You can download our worksheet at:

lqbook.co/resources

THIS IS ONLY THE BEGINNING

When we first sat down to write this book, we knew that we wanted to share a message that would help propel our industry to the next level. Looking back, ten years ago, testing was considered an afterthought or a bottleneck. Now, it has evolved into a discipline and has been refined to a point where we can have strategic conversations around testing and quality.

As you go on your own personal journey as a leader, we hope that this book acts as inspiration and as a guide for you to lead and influence your organizations and the wider testing community.

We've created the Leading Quality community on Slack (**lqbook.co/slack**) as a place to further these discussions, share best practice, and help quality leaders connect with each other. If you ever want to reach out to us personally, you can email us at:

- **ronald@leadingqualitybook.com**
- **owais@leadingqualitybook.com**

We look forward to hearing how this book has helped you and how you're helping others create better digital experiences for the world.

BONUS CHAPTER: THE FUTURE – AUTONOMOUS TESTING

A book about leading quality wouldn't be complete without taking a look at what the future holds. We believe that in the future, the QA industry will be heavily influenced by autonomous testing. The path toward autonomous testing involves reducing the effort and uncertainty of manual intervention in the QA process.

But how do we get there, and what effect will it have on the world of QA and software development? We have written a bonus chapter that examines what the future of test creation, maintenance, and execution looks like.

You can download this chapter at:

lqbook.co/bonus

HELP US PROMOTE THE MESSAGE OF LEADING QUALITY

If you liked this book and think it's something that others should be reading, you can help us in two ways:

1. Write an honest review on Amazon/Goodreads.
   Go to **lqbook.co/reviews**
2. Buy this book for your team. If you would like to buy more than ten copies, email us at **orders@leadingqualitybook.com** for a special discount.

KEY RESOURCES

WORKSHEETS

Head over to our online resources section to view our worksheets on:

- Creating your quality narrative
- How to work out your growth metric
- Setting vision for you and your team
- QA strategy questions

lqbook.co/resources

RESOURCES BY CHAPTER

Chapter 2 – The Power of a Quality Narrative

The Tipping Point: How Little Things Can Make a Big Difference – Malcolm Gladwell

Chapter 3 – Leading a Culture of Quality

Influence: The Psychology of Persuasion – Robert B. Cialdini

Whoever Tells the Best Story Wins: How to Use Your Own Stories to Communicate with Power and Impact – Annette Simmons

To Sell Is Human: The Surprising Truth About Moving Others – Daniel H. Pink

Thank You for Arguing: What Aristotle, Eminem and Homer (Simpson) Can Teach Us About the Art of Persuasion – Jay Heinrichs

Chapter 4 - Foundations: Manual Testing vs Automation

A Context-Driven Approach to Automation in Testing - James Bach & Michael Bolton

Chapter 5 – How Quality Changes with Product Maturity

Working Effectively with Legacy Code – Michael Feathers

Chapter 6 – Improving Feedback Loops to Supercharge Continuous Testing

Atomic Habits: An Easy & Proven Way to Build Good Habits & Break Bad Ones – James Clear

Ashley Hunsberger's *Transforming Culture with DevOps Pricipals* presentation has a great walkthrough on how to map your testing over your development pipeline.

https://github.com/ahunsberger/TransformingCulture

Chapter 7 – Investing in Testing Infrastructure

The Effective Engineer: How to Leverage Your Efforts in Software Engineering to Make a Disproportionate and Meaningful Impact – Edmond Lau

Continuous Delivery: Reliable Software Releases through Build, Test, and Deployment Automation – Jez Humble

The DevOps Handbook: How to Create World-Class Agility, Reliability, and Security in Technology Organizations – Gene Kim, Jez Humble, Patrick Debois & John Willis

Distributed Systems Observability – Cindy Sridharan

Chapter 8 – Connecting Your Quality Team to Business Growth

Measure What Matters: OKRs: The Simple Idea that Drives 10x Growth – John Doerr

Hacking Growth: How Today's Fastest-Growing Companies Drive Breakout Success – Sean Ellis

Chapter 10 – Leading Quality Strategy

The Hard Thing About Hard Things: Building a Business When There Are No Easy Answers – Ben Horowitz

Start with Why: How Great Leaders Inspire Everyone to Take Action – Simon Sinek

Find Your Why: A Practical Guide for Discovering Purpose for You and Your Team – Simon Sinek

Your Best Year Ever: A 5-Step Plan for Achieving Your Most Important Goals – Michael Hyatt

Sprint: How to Solve Big Problems and Test New Ideas in Just Five Days – Jake Knapp

RECOMMENDED BLOGS/INFLUENCERS

Rich Archbold - https://www.intercom.com/blog/

Dan Ashby - https://danashby.co.uk

James Bach - https://www.satisfice.com

Michael Bolton - https://www.developsense.com

Katrina Clokie - http://katrinatester.blogspot.com

Sean Ellis - https://growthhackers.com

Ashley Hunsberger - https://github.com/ahunsberger

Steve Janaway - http://stephenjanaway.co.uk

Will Larson - https://lethain.com

Edmond Lau - http://www.effectiveengineer.com/blog

Michael Lopp - https://randsinrepose.com/

Matt Newkirk - https://mattnewkirk.com/

ABOUT THE AUTHORS

Ronald Cummings-John and Owais Peer are the cofounders of Global App Testing (www.globalapptesting.com). Focusing on autonomous testing augmented with humans, Global App Testing allows teams to test in over 105 countries with 25,000 vetted professionals using real devices in real environments. This enables the company's customers to deliver high-quality products with minimal testing effort.

Hundreds of leading brands rely on Global App Testing's impact-first approach to quality, allowing Agile and DevOps teams to release faster and more often. Global App Testing was selected as one of the UK's fastest-growing technology companies.

Ronald and Owais have gained worldwide recognition for innovations in the testing field—most notably inventing Testathon® (www.testathon.co). Testathon® are hackathons for testers, which have been run in over 50 countries with leading tech teams from the likes of King, Spotify, and Instagram.

Both Ronald and Owais are highly sought-after speakers and advisors on QA and entrepreneurship. To book them for guest appearances on a podcast or to speak at your event,
contact **media@leadingqualitybook.com.**

ACKNOWLEDGEMENTS

"If I have seen further than others, it is by standing upon the
shoulders of giants."
Sir Isaac Newton

Developing a book is similar to developing a product. It requires interviews to ensure "book-market" fit, a diverse team coming together to make sure the content is right, and beta releases with the ideal reader (customer) to ensure it's providing value.

First, we have to thank the whole Global App Testing family for helping bring this book together. In particular Fahim Sachedina, who picked us up when we were stuck, project-managed, and supported the development of the ideas in this book as if it were his own. Nick Roberts for his drive to get this book completed and management of the whole team along the way. Tom Bransby for helping us get unstuck when we couldn't find the right words in the final days. Our research team Saskia Mathias, Emily Oswald, and Vanita Patel for getting all the little things done behind the scenes.

To our mentor and coach Derek Lewis, who stuck with us through all of the iterations and changes over the past few years. Thank you. Your energy and motivation to get this over the line have been nothing but inspiring.

To Jumee and the team at UMD International recording studio for their relentless performance coaching to ensure that we had an incredible audio version of this book.

To Vernon Richards, our incredible Testathon® host, who pushed us to write this book when it was a seed of an idea. Thank you for being there to bounce ideas off and sharpen our thinking when it comes to testing and quality. Also thank you for all the introductions you made to so many incredible people in the QA industry.

To Hugo Steckelmacher, our proofreader, you have an eye for detail unlike anyone we have ever met, thank you for being with us over all these years.

To Neil Brown for taking the time to write the foreword and being inspirational every time we sat down and talked about the future of our industry.

To Charles Adeeko, Dmitry Alexeenko, Dan Ashby, Dominic Assirati, Abby Bangser, Sally Goble, Ashley Hunsberger, Stephen Janaway, Mike Jones, Edmond Lau, Meaghan Lewis, Arylee McSweaney, Shesh Patel, and Ilya Sakharov, whose stories made it into the final draft. Your openness in sharing your experiences is what made this book special.

To Klaas Ardinois, Fab Avila, James Bach, Richard Bengtsson, Michael Bolton, Nick Caldwell, Cliff Chang, Katrina Clokie, Adam Dunkley, Sean Ellis, Fred Esere, Dominic Feargrieve James, Luís Franqueira, Arjun Gadhia, Tom Gardiner, Mauricio Giacomello, Luca Grulla, Ethan Gui, Aaron Haehn, Pam Hernandez, Marty Hoevenberg, Alexandra Hoffer, Mark Hrynczak, Bilal Khan, Rik Marselis, Geoff Meyer, Matthew Newkirk, Minette Norman, Steve Odlind, Simon Prior, Niranjan Ravichandran, Filipe Rodriguez, Kevin Roulleau, Robert Shaw, Lidia Sinitsyna, Gordon Skinner, Suyash Sonwalkar, Douglas Squirrel, Tom Stoffer, Leonidas Tsementzis, Simon Turvey, Ajay Varia, Robert Watts, Gerald Weinberg, Daniel Wiskman, Eoin Woods, Qasar Younis, and Julien Lavigne du Cadet for your contributions, inspiration, and feedback during the writing of this book.

To James Bach, Amber Brocato, Lisa Crispin, Franck Halegoi, Daniel Knott, Tobias Kreuzig, Michael Lopp, Robert C. Martin, James Meddock, Janine Percucello, Kevin Pyles, Roza Romanova, and Jas Singh for reading drafts of the book and providing valuable feedback on the manuscript.

And finally, to you, for taking the time to read this book.

Thank you.

NOTES

In this section, we list the many sources that we have used and referenced in this book. However, we acknowledge that ideas are fluid and people often build on others' ideas. There may be cases where we have (unintentionally) made a mistake by attributing an idea to the wrong person or not giving credit to someone where due.

If you believe we have made a mistake, feel free to email us at **bugs@ leadingqualitybook.com**, so that we can make any corrections as soon as possible.

We'll be keeping a full list of the updated endnotes and corrections at **lqbook.co/resources**.

1   "Sukarno, Suharto, Megawati: Why Do Some Indonesians Have Only One Name?" *International Business Times*, September 19, 2013, https://www.ibtimes.com/sukarno-suharto-megawati-why-do-some-indonesians-have-only-one-name-1408204.

2   Michael Bolton's definition expands on Jerry Weinberg's original definition that, "Quality is value to some person." "What is Quality?" *Flow of Testing*, May 26, 2014, https://flowoftesting.wordpress.com/2014/05/26/what-is-quality/.

3   Amazon's "Annual Letter to Shareholders 2018," SEC, April 18, 2018, https://www.sec.gov/Archives/edgar/data/1018724/000119312518121161/d456916dex991.htm

4   "Why Software Testing is Key to DevOps," *TechWell*, February 9, 2018, https://www.techwell.com/techwell-insights/2018/02/why-software-testing-key-devops.

5   "Testing Trends for 2018, A Survey of Development and Testing Professionals."

Sauce Labs, February, 2018, https://cdn.agilitycms.com/sauce-labs/white-papers/sauce-labs-state-of-testing-2018.pdf.

6   Ibid.—adapted from the diagram on page 11.

7   Ibid.

8   "Software Fail Watch: 5th Edition," Tricentis, June 1, 2019, https://www.tricentis.com/resources/software-fail-watch-5th-edition.

9   "Up to 300k NHS Heart Patients May Have Been Given Wrong Drugs," *Health Medicine Network*, May 11, 2016, http://healthmedicinet.com/i2/up-to-300k-nhs-heart-patients-may-have-been-given-wrong-drugs.

10 "WHOOPS: American Airlines Without Pilots for Christmas After Scheduling System Glitch," CNBC, November 29, 2017, https://www.cnbc.com/2017/11/29/thousands-of-american-airlines-flights-dont-have-scheduled-pilots-union.html.

11 "Bad Data and New IT System Bugs Help Knock Off 66% Off Provident Financial Share Price," *The Register*, August 23, 2017, https://www.theregister.co.uk/2017/08/23/provident_financial_software_woes_share_price_crash.

12 "Software Fail Watch: 5th Edition," Tricentis, June 1, 2019, https://www.tricentis.com/resources/software-fail-watch-5th-edition

13 Mike Jones, conversations with the authors.

14 *Entrepreneur Voices on Company Culture.*

15 "Snapchat has a huge problem with Android, and it's causing investors to worry,"*Business Insider*, February 21, 2017, https://www.businessinsider.com/snapchat-huge-problem-with-android-causing-investors-to-worry-2017-2?r=US&IR=T.

16 Arylee McSweaney, conversations with the authors.

17 Shesh Patel, conversations with the authors.

18 "The Freaky Friday Management Technique," Andreessen Horowitz, January 19,

2012, https://a16z.com/2012/01/19/the-freaky-friday-management-technique.

19   "How Designers Work With Developers: A round up [sic] of interviews on how product designers collaborate with developers,"*Medium*, April 29, 2017, https://uxdesign.cc/how-designers-work-with-developers-7552be5e40e9.

20   "How Designers and Developers Can Pair Together to Create Better Products," *Medium*, June 22, 2017. https://medium.com/product-labs/how-designers-and-developers-can-pair-together-to-create-better-products-e4b09e3ca096.

21   "Quality Assistance: How Atlassian Does QA," Atlassian, https://www.atlassian.com/inside-atlassian/qa.

22   "Testing at Airbnb," *Medium,* February 27, 2014, https://medium.com/airbnb-engineering/testing-at-airbnb-199f68a0a40d.

23   This is Robert B. Cialdini's sixth principle of influence. His book *Influence* is a great read to understand the psychology of persuasion.

24   Surname and company details omitted for confidentiality reasons.

25   "World Quality Report 2018-19," Capgemini, https://www.capgemini.com/service/world-quality-report-2018-19.

26   "Edward Bernays, 'Father of Public Relations' and Leader in Opinion Making, Dies at 103," *New York Times*, March 10, 1995: http://movies2.nytimes.com/books/98/08/16/specials/bernays-obit.html.

27   By *Life* magazine, as reported here: "American Decades of the 20th Century: Life Magazine Lists 20th Century's Most Influential Americans," Timberlane, October 25, 2018, https://libguides.timberlane.net/c.php?g=464885&p=3192709.

28   "Continuous Testing in DevOps" Dan Ashby, October 19, 2016, https://danashby.co.uk/2016/10/19/continuous-testing-in-devops/.

29 The model used in this book has been edited and simplified from the one Dan originally shared during a conversation with the authors. The original version that Dan shared can be found on his website, "Information, and its relationship with testing and checking," Dan Ashby, March 8, 2016, https://danashby.co.uk/2016/03/08/information-and-its-relationship-with-testing-and-checking.
  Dan's framework has its foundation in Michael Bolton and James Bach's work titled "A Context-Driven Approach to Automation in Testing" (https://www.satisfice.com/download/a-context-driven-approach-to-automation-in-testing).
  In this book, the terms "Investigating" and "Verifying" have been used instead of the original "testing" and "checking."

30 "Reducing the Cost of IT Automations—Is Automation Always the Answer?" Usenix, https://www.usenix.org/legacy/event/hotos05/final_papers/full_papers/brown/brown.pdf.

31 Based on the "Diffusion of Innovation Theory," as discussed in the following article: BUMC, August 29, 2018, http://sphweb.bumc.bu.edu/otlt/MPH-Modules/SB/BehavioralChangeTheories/BehavioralChangeTheories4.html.

32 "Why Product Owners Should Care About Quality" *Roman Pichler,* April 8, 2010, https://www.romanpichler.com/blog/why-product-owners-should-care-about-quality/.

33 "About Us," King, https://discover.king.com/about.

34 Dominic Assirati, conversations with the authors.

35 "Dogfooding" is a term referring to when a company uses its own product.

36 "Google Maps: 1 Billion Monthly Users," *GPS Business News*, July 17, 2014, https://gpsbusinessnews.com/Google-Maps-1-Billion-Monthly-Users_a4964.html.

37 "The Rise and Fall of Knight Capital — Buy High, Sell Low. Rinse and Repeat." *Medium*, August 5, 2018, https://hackernoon.com/the-rise-and-fall-of-knight-capital-buy-high-sell-low-rinse-and-repeat-ae17fae780f6.

38 Ashley Hunsberger, conversations with the authors.

39 You can see Ashley's example in the YouTube video of her talk "Transform Culture Using DevOps Principles:" https://www.youtube.com/watch?v=RBrAj9jKgX0&t=1627s.

40 Capers Jones, *Applied Software Measurement*; Marco Morana, "Building Security into the Software Life Cycle."

41 There is a lot of debate around the measurement of the costs in this study. For an excellent read, see *The Leprechauns of Software Engineering* by Laurent Bossavit.

42 Ibid.

43 See Dan Ashby's great article titled "Continuous Testing in DevOps." Dan Ashby, October 19, 2016, https://danashby.co.uk/2016/10/19/continuous-testing-in-devops.

44 Table adapted from Elisabeth's talk: https://www.youtube.com/watch?v=F0BRsnYwnBk&t=987s.

45 Charles Adeeko, conversations with the authors.

46 "My Philosophy on Alerting: based on my observations while I was a Site Reliability Engineer at Google," http://files.catwell.info/misc/mirror/rob-ewaschuk-google-sre-philosophy-alerting.pdf.

47 Ibid. Edited for clarity.

48 "Symptom-Based Monitoring at Ticketmaster," Ticketmaster, August 19, 2015, https://tech.ticketmaster.com/2015/08/19/symptom-based-monitoring-at-ticketmaster.

49 Ibid.

50 Sally Goble, conversations with the authors.

51 "Testing in Production, the safe way," *Medium*, March 25, 2018, https://medium.com/@copyconstruct/testing-in-production-the-safe-way-18ca102d0ef1.

52 "The Servers Are Burning,"*Logic Magazine*, August 2018, https://logicmag.io/05-the-servers-are-burning.

53 Meaghan Lewis, conversations with the authors.

54 "Engineering Metrics: Grow Your Business with Outcomes, Not Activity," OpenView Venture Partners, August 10, 2016, https://openviewpartners.com/blog/engineering-metrics/#.XQZaVtNKiL4.

55 Name and company details omitted for confidentiality reasons.

56 Ilya Sakharov, conversations with the authors.

57 To find out more about OKRs, read *Measure What Matters* by John Doerr.

58 "Social Media Fact Sheet" *Pew Research Center*, June 12, 2019, https://www.pewinternet.org/fact-sheet/social-media/

59 "Every Product Needs a North Star Metric: Here's How to Find Yours," Amplitude, March 21, 2018, https://amplitude.com/blog/2018/03/21/product-north-star-metric.

60 "How Netflix Measures Success," *Business Insider*, February 1, 2016, http://uk.businessinsider.com/netflixs-most-important-metric-2016-2.

61 "How Slack Became The Fastest-Growing Enterprise Software Ever," *Forbes*, November 11, 2018, https://www.forbes.com/sites/johnkoetsier/2018/11/30/how-slack-became-the-fastest-growing-enterprise-software-ever/#6c04556e7aed.

62 "From 0 to $1B – Slack's Founder Shares Their Epic Launch Strategy," First Round, https://firstround.com/review/From-0-to-1B-Slacks-Founder-Shares-Their-Epic-Launch-Strategy.

63 To understand more about creating growth metrics, I'd advise you to look at Sean Ellis' work on what he calls "North Star Metrics," *Medium*, June 5, 2017, https://blog.growthhackers.com/what-is-a-north-star-metric-b31a8512923f.

64 "Sean Ellis on charting a path toward sustainable growth," Intercom, June 7, 2018, https://www.intercom.com/blog/podcasts/sean-ellis-growth.

65 Dmitry Alexeenko, conversations with the authors.

66 "South Korea's Online Banking System Is Stuck in 1996," *Forbes*, November 30,

2016, https://www.forbes.com/sites/elaineramirez/2016/11/30/south-koreas-online-banking-system-is-stuck-in-1996/#53648374527c.

67 These are examples of the personas used by marketing automation company HubSpot.

68 "How GoDaddy Launched in 125 Countries in 3 Years: An Interview with James Carroll, EVP of Global Platform Development," OneSky, June 12, 2017, http://www.oneskyapp.com/blog/godaddy-international-growth-strategy.

69 "The Inside Story on How SurveyMonkey Cracked the International Market," First Round, https://firstround.com/review/the-inside-story-on-how-surveymonkey-cracked-the-international-market.

70 "Why millions of people are helping Google build the most accurate Maps in the world," *Business Insider*, September 14, 2016, http://uk.businessinsider.com/google-maps-local-guides-2016-9.

71 "Google Maps' futuristic AR walking navigation is now in testing by Level 5+ Local Guides," *Android Police*, February 28, 2019, https://www.androidpolice.com/2019/02/28/google-maps-futuristic-ar-walking-navigation-is-now-in-testing-by-level-5-local-guides.

72 "Why Vision is More Important than Strategy," Michael Hyatt, January 23, 2012, https://michaelhyatt.com/why-vision-is-more-important-than-strategy.

73 Ibid.

74 "How great leaders inspire action," TED, September 2009, https://www.ted.com/talks/simon_sinek_how_great_leaders_inspire_action?language=en.

75 Napoleon Hill, *Think and Grow Rich*.

INDEX

3Cs:
    career impact, 13 - 15
    company issues, 13 - 17
    customer issues, 13 - 17
    description and explanation of, 13
    guide teams and colleagues in a way that
    positively impacts, 15 - 16
    improvement in the, 16
    the effects of poor quality on, 13 - 15

A
A/B Testing, 85
Accelerate growth:
    alignment of teams, 86
    leveraging quality teams, 3
localization, 95
Acceptance testing, 66figt
ActiveX, 94
Adeeko, Charles, 71 *see also*: EVRYTHNG
Agile:
    development, 11
    practices, 61, 71
Airbnb:
    localization, 93 - 94
    quality culture, 38
supporting quality narratives with internal
evidence, 36
    transaction based growth metrics, 88
Alexeenko, Dmitry, 91
Alignment:
    company culture, 32 - 39
    inter-departmental relationships, 85 - 86
Amazon:
    continuous delivery, 72 - 73
    customer satisfaction, 6
American Airlines, 13, 25

Amplitude, 87
Analytics,
    growth metrics, 87 - 89
    internal analytics, 96
Android:
    proprietary operating systems, 96
    quality issues, 21
AppDynamics, 96
Apple: 11
    iOs, 21
    Steve Jobs, 11, 93
App:
    bugs, 13, 42, 58
    growth, 21
    infrastructure, 56
    localization, 97
Ashby, Dan: 45, 65 *see also*: eBay
Assirati, Dominic: 53
Atlassian: 35 - 38
Attention based growth metrics, 87, 92 *see also*:
Growth Metrics
Audience:
    identifying who to influence, 32 - 39
Automation:
    automation script, 47
    automation suite, 61, 84
    can you automate everything, 45 - 47
    development, 45
    reduce QA bottleneck, 41 - 44
    should you automate everything, 48 - 49
    test, 30, 48, 54 - 57, 63
    UwI, 71

B

B2B (business-to-business), 54, 88, 92
B2C (business-to-consumer), 78, 87, 92
Bangser, Abby, 68
Bebo, 52
Benchmark, 53 - 54, 97
Bernays, Edward, 43
Beta users, 55, 98 - 99
Blackboard, 60 - 67 *see also*: Hunsberger, Ashley
Blasse, Nikkel, 35
Bloom & Wild, 56
Bottleneck, 12, 41, 107
Bug:
    continuous deployment, 11 - 14
    continuous testing, 63, 68
    customer experience, 42, 55
    growth metric, 83 - 84, 90
    localization, 1 - 4, 99
    zero bugs, 82
Buffett, Warren, 24
Business:
    growth, 3 - 5, 91
    metric, 83 - 84, 90
    outcomes, 16, 84

C

Canary release, 77
Cancel, David, 22
Candy Crush, 53
Code:
    codebase, 14, 56, 59 - 62, 85
    continuous delivery, 72 - 79
    development, 11, 54 - 56, 62, 85
    exploratory testing techniques, 35
    feedback loops, 65
    testing, 36 - 37
    legacy software, 58
Cohen, Jason, 19
Communication, 5, 35, 54, 7, 85
Company growth metric, 82- 92
Company issues, 13 *see also*: 3Cs
Continuous integration, 62, 72
Continuous testing:
    definition, 63
    development cycle, 64
    feedback loops, 61 - 70
Core metric, 25, 76, 82 - 88
Cross-functional teamwork, 22, 85, 90
Crowdsourced testing, 57, 68, 99
Culture:
    culture problems, 19
    quality culture, 20, 31, 44, 62
    team, 43
Customer:
    acquisition, 93- 94, 107
    empathy, 98
    issues, 13 *see also*: 3Cs
    expectations, 54 - 58
    support, 34, 73, 91, 93

D

DAU (Daily Active Users), 87, 90
Data:
    external, 37
    growth metrics, 85
    internal, 36, 74, 96
    user, 73
Delivery pipeline, 71
Designers, 22, 35
DevOps, 45, 61, 64
Development velocity, 41
DeviceAtlas, 97
Diverse:
    user experience, 95
    viewpoints when achieving
    alignment, 34
Dogfooding, 54, 77
Dr. Sigmund Freud, 43

E

eBay, 45 *see also*: Dan Ashby
E-commerce, 88, 104
EVRYTHNG, 71, 79 *see also*: Charles Adeeko
Early adopters, 52, 54
Ellis, Sean, 90
Empathy engineering, 93
Engineering: 40, 58 - 60, 130
    culture, 30
    empathy, 93
    leaders, 19
    sales, 34
Environment:
    company culture, 14
    development, 24
    testing, 73 - 75, 94, 97 - 100
Etsy, 30 - 31 *see also*: Arylee McSweaney
Existing users, 57, 98
Expansion, 96, 108
Exploratory testing, 35, 44 - 47, 55 - 56, 66
External evidence, 37

F

Feathers, Michael, 59
Features:
    delivering, 71
    developing new, 14, 33, 42, 56, 79, 82, 93 - 95
    reworking, 26, 74
Feedback Loop:
automation, 49
explanation, 64
    improving, 61, 67 - 68, 110figt
    infrastructure, 98
Functional testing, 1

G

Github, 79 *see also*: Meaghan Lewis
Global:
    growth, 1, 13, 94
    market, 94
Global App Testing, 4, 51
Goble, Sally, 76
GoDaddy, 95
Google:
    analytics, 96
    maps, 57 - 58, 99
    play, 21
Growth hacking, 90
Growth metric:

attention-based, 87, 92
choosing your growth metric, 87
company growth metric, 25
core metric, 76, 82 - 83, 88,
transaction-based, 88, 92, 108
productivity-based, 88, 92, 108
Grove, Andy, 85

H

HelloFresh, 85 - 86
Hendrickson, Elisabeth, 65
Hill, Napoleon, 111
Horowitz, Ben, 34
How to Test Narrative, 23 - 29
HubSpot, 22
Hunsberger, Ashley, 61
Hyatt, Michael, 103

I

IBM, 48
iHeartMedia, 55
Impact-driven methodology, 74
Indonesia, 1 - 2, 25
Indus OS, 96
Influence:
    audience, 32
    persuade, 38, 44, 109figt
    quality narrative, 32
Infrastructure:
    automation, 43
    costs, 26, 37, 79
    development, 85, 105
    feedback loops, 67 - 69
    predictability, 52, 55 - 60
    QA, 53
    testing, 71 - 80, 98
Innovators, 52
Instagram, 21
Intel, 85
Internal:
analytics, 96
    communication, 22, 35, 85, 90
    company culture, 20, 31, 43 - 44, 62
    data, 36, 74, 96
    dogfooding, 54, 77
    evidence, 36-37
Internet Explorer, 94

J
Janaway, Steve, 56
Jira, 35
Jobs, Steve, 11, 93
Jones, Capers, 63
Jones, Mike, 15, 86

K
Kagen, Noah, 86
Kaizen, 11
King, 53
Kim, Gene, 64
Knight Capital, 58
Kosak, Lou, 36
KPIs (Key Performance Indicator), 16

L
Laggards, 52 - 53
Late majority, 52
Lau, Edmond, 72 *see also*: The Effective Engineer
Lead quality, 5 - 8, 39, 91, 103, 111
Leadership team, 33, 86
Lean principles, 11
Legacy software, 58
Lewis, Meaghan, 78
Lineage OS, 97
Local:
    experience, 97
    guides, 99
    persona, 93 - 98, 108
    testing, 1, 94 - 98, 108
Location:
    customer experience, 95
    devices, 57
    testing, 94 - 98, 108
LogMeIn, 90
Lyft, 88

M
MOO: 68
MTTR (Mean Time to Recover), 89
Manual testing, 41 - 50, 55
Market:
    global, 94, 97
    local, 95, 99
    marketplaces, 65, 88
    product market fit, 11, 53, 107

testing vendors, 44
Marketing, 90 - 95
Match.com, 54
Maxim, Mike, 78
McSweaney, Arylee, 30 *see also*: Etsy
Medium, 77
Microsoft, 4, 74, 94
Monitoring:
    continuous testing, 73
    impact on users, 73 - 79
    symptom-based, 73 - 75
Motivation, 14, 32, 39, 85, 105
MySpace, 52

N
National Health Service, 13
Nelson Books, 102
Netflix, 87- 88

O
OKCupid, 78
OKRs (Objectives and Key Results), 85 - 86
Onboarding experience, 96
OpenSignal, 97
Outcome-led metric, 83, 91
Ownership narrative, 20 - 29, 71, 83, 107

P
Patel, Shesh, 33
Personal vision, 104 - 106
Pink, Daniel, 31
Pivotal Labs, 35, 65
Poor quality, 13 - 18
Predictability, 52, 55, 57, 60, 107
Procter & Gamble, 33
Product:
    management, 85
    market fit, 52 - 60
    maturity, 24, 51, 53, 58, 107
Productivity-based growth metric, 88, 92, 108
Provident Financial, 14
Public relations, 43

Q

Quality:
advocates, 38
assurance, 84
bottleneck, 41
narrative, 19, 27 - 29
standards, 10
strategy, 7 - 8, 102 - 111
Quality Narrative:
the 'how to test' narrative, 23 - 29
the ownership narrative, 20 - 29, 71, 83, 107
the value narrative, 20, 24, 29, 110
Quora, 72

R

ROI (Return On Investment), 20, 25, 29
Reddit, 4, 21
Reeves, Martin, 23
Regression testing, 57
Retention, 26, 91, 96, 108
Revenue potential, 25 - 27, 110
Richards, Vernon, 45
Ries, Eric, 83
Risk-based analysis, 85
Risk mitigation, 27

S

Sakharov, Ilya, 85 - 86
Sauce Labs, 12, 68
Scalable, 53, 98
Sinek, Simon, 104
Slack, 74, 88 - 89
Snapchat, 21
Social networks, 35, 52
Social media, 21, 52
Software development cycle, 63
Software development, 6, 24, 31, 63
Spiegel, Evan, 21
Spotify, 38
Sridharan, Cindy, 77
Stack Overflow, 34
Stakeholder feedback, 38
Starbucks, 58
Startup, 3 - 4, 15, 51, 82
Support function, 83 - 84
SurveyMonkey, 97

T

TQM (Total Quality Management), 11
Teams, 21
cross-functional relationships, 85 - 86
ownership narrative, 21, 22
quality, 30, 42
Team Skill and Capacity, 110figt
Teamwork, 90
Test strategies, 85
Testing:
A/B Testing, 85
acceptance testing, 66figt
automation, 30, 48, 54 - 57, 63
automation UI, 71
code testing, 36 - 37
crowdsourced testing, 57, 68, 99
exploratory testing, 35, 44 - 47, 55 - 56, 66
functional, 1
infrastructure, 71 - 80, 98
local, 1, 94 - 98, 108
manual, 41 - 50, 55
regression, 57
Testing in production, 70 - 78
The Effective Engineer (Lau), 72
The Freaky Friday Management Technique, 34
The Guardian, 75 - 79
The Lean Startup (Ries), 83
The New York Times, 33, 103
The Phoenix Project, 64
Thomas Nelson publishing, 102
Ticketmaster, 73 - 74
Tinder, 54
Tizen OS, 97
To Sell is Human (Pink), 31
Transaction-based growth metrics, 88, 92, 108
Twitter, 34

U

UI automation, 71
Uber, 58, 88
Unit test, 23 - 25, 54, 58, 66
User experience, 22, 42, 55
User persona, 94
uSwitch, 15 - 16, 86

V

Validation, 31, 52 - 59, 60, 107
Value narrative, 20, 24, 29, 110
Vanity metrics, 83
Verifying, 46 - 47
Virtual reality, 82
Vision:
    company, 102- 106
    department, 106
    personal, 104 - 106
Vivo, 94

W

Walter, Andy, 33
Waterfall, 61
WP Engine, 19
Wizz Air, 90
Working Effectively with Legacy Code
(Feathers), 59

Z

Zero bugs, 82 - 83
ZTE, 94
Zynga, 34